CONTENTS

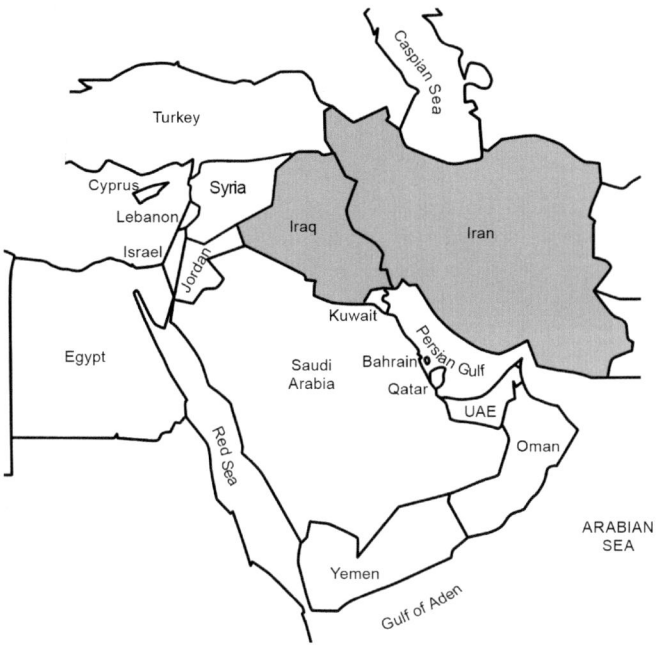

Abbreviations
Preface and Acknowledgements

1   Setting the Scene
2   The Mother of Military Build-ups   13
3   Iraq's Naval Reaction   29
4   Crisis and Escalation   36
5   The Opening Round   41
6   Organising Caravans   50
7   The Iraqi Medusa   57

Appendix
Ships trapped in the Shatt al-Arab, September–October 1980   63

Sources and Bibliography   65
Notes   67
About the Authors   70

Note

In order to simplify the use of this book, all names, locations and geographic designations are as provided in The Times World Atlas, or other traditionally accepted major sources of reference, as of the time of the described events. Similarly, Arabic names are romanised and transcripted rather than transliterated. For example: the definite article al- before words starting with 'sun letters' is given as pronounced instead of simply as al- (which is the usual practice for non-Arabic speakers in most English-language literature and media). For the reasons of space, ranges – which are usually measured in feet and nautical miles in international aeronautics – are cited in metric measurements only.

Helion & Company Limited
Unit 8 Amherst Business Centre, Budbrooke Road, Warwick CV34 5WE, England
Tel. 01926 499 619
Email: info@helion.co.uk   Website: www.helion.co.uk   Twitter: @helionbooks   Visit our blog http://blog.helion.co.uk/

Published by Helion & Company 2023
Designed and typeset by Farr out Publications, Wokingham, Berkshire
Cover designed by Paul Hewitt, Battlefield Design (www.battlefield-design.co.uk)

Text © Tom Cooper, E. R. Hooton and Sirous Ebrahimi 2023
Photographs © as individually credited
Colour profiles © Luca Canossa, Ivan Zajac and Tom Cooper 2023
Maps © Tom Cooper and Micky Hewitt 2023

Every reasonable effort has been made to trace copyright holders and to obtain their permission for the use of copyright material. The author and publisher apologise for any errors or omissions in this work, and would be grateful if notified of any corrections that should be incorporated in future reprints or editions of this book.

ISBN 978-1-914377-20-4

British Library Cataloguing-in-Publication Data.
A catalogue record for this book is available from the British Library.

All rights reserved. No part of this publication may be reproduced, stored in a retrieval system, or transmitted, in any form, or by any means, electronic, mechanical, photocopying, recording or otherwise, without the express written consent of Helion & Company Limited.

For details of other military history titles published by Helion & Company Limited contact the above address, or visit our website: http://www.helion.co.uk. We always welcome receiving book proposals from prospective authors.

ABBREVIATIONS

AB	air base
ABOT	al-Basra Oil Terminal (Iraq)
AIOC	Anglo-Iranian Oil Company (formerly Anglo-Persian Oil Company, later BP)
ASCC	Air Standardisation Coordinating Committee
ASW	Anti-Submarine Warfare
ASWS	Anti-Submarine Warfare Squadron
BARCAP	barrier combat air patrol
BIK	Bandar-e Khomeini
CENTO	Central Treaty Organization
Chaff	reflective jamming device made up of thin, lightweight metallic strips, cut to one-half length of the target's radar wavelength
dwt	deadweight tonnage; a measure of the carrying capacity of a ship
ECM	electronic countermeasures
ESMCP	Emergency Shipping Movement Control Plan for the Persian Gulf (IRIN)
FAC	Fast attack craft
grt	Gross Registered Tonnage; a measure of the cubic capacity of a ship
IFF	Identification Friend or Foe
I-HAWK	Improved Homing-All-The-Way Killer (US-made SAM)
IIAF	Imperial Iranian Air Force
IIN	Imperial Iranian Navy
IINS	Imperial Iranian Navy Ship
IrAAC	Iraq Army Aviation Corps
IrAF	Iraq Air Force (official designation since 1958)
IRGC	Islamic Revolutionary Guards Corps (Iran)
IRIAA	Islamic Republic of Iran Army Aviation
IRIAF	Islamic Republic of Iran Air Force
IRIN	Islamic Republic of Iran Navy
IRINA	Islamic Republic of Iran Naval Aviation
IRINS	Islamic Republic of Iran Navy Ship
KAAOT	Khowr al-Amiya Oil Terminal (Iraq)
MANPAD	man-portable air defence system (shoulder-fired anti-aircraft missile)
MiG	Mikoyan i Gurevich (the design bureau led by Artyom Ivanovich Mikoyan and Mikhail Iosifovich Gurevich, also known as OKB-155 or MMZ 'Zenit')
NATO	North Atlantic Treaty Organization
NIOC	National Iranian Oil Company
OPEC	Organization of Petroleum Exporting Countries
PMO	Port and Maritime Organisation (Iran)
RAF	Royal Air Force (base) (of Great Britain)
RIO	radar intercept officer (back-seater in the F-14A Tomcat)
SAM	surface-to-air missile
SAR	search and rescue
SAVAMA	*Sezeman-e Ettalaat va Amniat-e Keshvar* (Intelligence and Security Organisation of the Country; reorganised SAVAK since 1979)
Su	Sukhoi (the design bureau led by Pavel Ossipovich Sukhoi, also known as OKB-51)
TFS	Tactical Fighter Squadron
USAF	United States Air Force
USN	US Navy
USSR	Union of Soviet Socialist Republics (also 'Soviet Union')

PREFACE AND ACKNOWLEDGEMENTS

The coming-into-being of this book was protracted and, often enough, problematic. During the Iran-Iraq War of 1980–88, hardly a month passed without the newspapers – and sometimes TV reports – mentioning one or another of the 'supertankers' underway in the Persian Gulf coming under attack from the Iranian or Iraqi armed forces. Generally, hardly any of these reports were to be found on the front pages of contemporary newspapers, and most only mentioned the name of the ship, and under what flag was it underway. Individually, most such attacks did not make much sense: there was no recognisable pattern behind them; the timing and locations at which they took place were unclear; and the ships attacked often flew the flag of very different nations. Only the 'big picture' was clear: there was a real naval war between Iran and Iraq going on.

On the other hand (and the reader is advised to mind that there was no internet at the time), the Falklands War fought by Argentina and Great Britain in 1982 was still much more often discussed – in the specialised press, at various conferences, and even in the 'squadron ready rooms' of the various air forces around the world – than the 'hard to cover' Iran-Iraq War. To a certain degree, and although colloquially known as the 'Gulf War', it appeared as if the Iran-Iraq War included no naval warfare component at all. It took time until even the best-connected sources within the specialised press began revealing at least some details: the majority of these were related to the French decision to lease five Dassault Super Etendard fighter-bombers – armed with Aérospatiale AM.39 Exocet anti-ship missiles – to Iraq, a country with next to no coast and 'such a small navy' that it was regularly ignored even by major sources of reference. Apparently, there was no naval war between Iran and Iraq at all…?

After earning themselves quite some reputation during the Falklands War, Super Etendards were announced as a major escalation in what soon became known as the 'Tanker War'. The latter was considered as a 'bi-product' of the often entirely irrational Iran-Iraq War that had been raging since September 1980. However, before long, related reporting stopped: on the contrary, reports began surfacing about Iraq operating Dassault Mirage F.1 fighters armed with Exocets instead. As the frequency of related reports continued to increase, they were ignored by the public until May 1987 when, one of the 'Iraqi Mirages' reportedly hit the US Navy frigate USS *Stark* (FFG-31) with two Exocets, killing 37 of the crew. During the following months, the media went head over heels into reporting from the Persian Gulf – but focused on accusations and counteraccusations about who was responsible for this attack, what it meant on the geo-strategic level, and what might happen in the future: once again, naval warfare between Iran and Iraq was largely ignored. This changed very little even as more than 50 warships of the US Navy, the Royal Navy of Great Britain, the French Navy, and the Soviet Navy entered the Persian Gulf – officially to protect international maritime trade. What followed over the next year were reports about several clashes between US and Iranian armed forces, culminating in the guided missile frigate USS *Samuel B Jones* (FFG-

58) hitting a mine allegedly laid by Iran, and the US Navy retaliating with Operation Praying Mantis of April 1988, when it sank two major Iranian warships. As 'the cherry on the cake', the US Navy guided missile cruiser USS *Vincennes* (CG-49) then shot down an Iran Air airliner in July of the same year. Soon after, the Iran-Iraq War was over, and almost everything of this was overshadowed by subsequent developments – and then quickly forgotten: apparently, if there *was* a naval war between Iran and Iraq, then it was only once the US Navy became involved....

During the late 1990s, and very slowly at first, some additional information began surfacing from Iran – usually emphasising heroic resistance of local heroes against an imposed war. Gradually, the number of reports published in the local press grew, but they were often spiced with mythology and little more than rumours. Instead, the first authoritative account about the naval warfare emerged in the West in the form of the book *Tanker War: The Assault on Merchant Shipping During the Iran-Iraq War*, by Martin S Navias and Edward R. Hooton. Largely based on a cross-examination of insurance-related reporting about losses of merchant shipping and Mr. Hooton's expertise in maritime affairs from when he worked for the specialist British publisher Jane's, this was the first book explaining the background and context of the naval war between Iran and Iraq, and as such: a true 'eyeopener'.

Still, much of the background and many details remained unclear, and it took another – and this time an even bigger, more dramatic, longer-lasting, and outright mind-boggling – tragedy to change the situation: the US-led invasion of Iraq in 2003 caused millions of Iraqis to flee abroad. Combined with the widespread use of the internet, this enabled the establishment of contact with Brigadier General Ahmad Sadik Rushdie al-Astrabadi, former officer of the Iraqi Air Force Intelligence Department, and an avid historian of the Iraqi Air Force (IrAF). Cooperation with him initiated the period of the first serious advances in research of the operational history of the Iraqi armed forces. Meanwhile, Western interest in experiences from the Iran-Iraq War caused a sort of 'mini-revolution' in publishing in the Islamic Republic of Iran: numerous Iranian researchers have during the 2000s published – extensively – about the Iranian armed forces at war with Iraq, and the situation eventually reached a point where veteran officers created think-tanks, specialised in research and publication about this conflict. Eventually, this enabled Farzin Nadimi to be granted special permission to work with official archive of the National Iranian Oil Company (NIOC) and similar authorities, resulting in the first authoritative account of one crucial aspect of the naval war between Iran and Iraq: the effects of Iraq's onslaught on the Iranian petrochemical industry – in the form of his PhD thesis upon that topic.

Unsurprisingly, considering the US-led invasion and a murderous civil war that ripped their country apart during the 2000s, Iraqis were slower to follow and have published much less. Even if, their top researchers – whether Brigadier General Astrabadi, or Ali al-Tobchi, an engineer involved in Project al-Hussein – were connected to the people, and thus the equipment and operational history, of the IrAF.[1] The Iraqi Navy was a relatively small service, much overlooked by almost everybody (starting with the authorities in Baghdad), and its activity was deeply overshadowed by gigantic campaigns fought between Iran and Iraq on the ground and in the air. Finally, while both Iranians and Iraqis are – invariably – generous and hospitable people, ready to go out of their way to cooperate, they are also deeply suspicious and morbidly sensitive, while the memory of participants – of whom there are ever fewer as the time passes by – is not improving. Rather unsurprisingly, over the last 10 years both sides rather excelled at creating ever further myths instead of focusing on facts: the net result is that almost everything published in one or the other country – no matter by whom – requires extensive and time-consuming cross-examination.

It is against this backdrop that research into the naval warfare between Iran and Iraq has remained problematic until the last few years, when Sirous Ebrahimi – a veteran of the Iran-Iraq War and a retired pilot of the Iranian merchant navy – embarked on research in the official archives of the Islamic Republic of Iran Navy (IRIN), the Islamic Republic of Iran Air Force (IRIAF), and the Port & Maritime Organisation (PMO). It was the results of his work that enabled the coming-into-being of this book: the first ever about the Iran-Iraq War in the English language largely based on official documentation.

In addition to the above-mentioned gentlemen and researchers, another impetus for this project was provided by *Ing*. Günther Jakowitch, an engineer from Austria who worked in Iraq for much of the 1980s, and who has strongly supported the research about Iraqi acquisition of Mirage F.1s and their operational deployment.[2] Last but not least, I would like to express my gratitude to Leon Manoucherians, editor of the *Iranian Aviation Review*, who has greatly supported this project with his knowledge and a rich collection of photographs; to Albert Grandolini, from France, who is continuously supporting all of my work with all of his powers; and to Milos Sipos, from Slovakia, for his help with a plethora of information on the Iraqi Air Force.

Rather unexpectedly, what eventually prompted the finalisation of years of research was a discussion related to the emergence of what is known as the Littoral Combat Ship, developed for the US Navy (USN) in the 2000s in reaction to experiences from involvement in several 'small/low-intensity wars' around the globe. In the course of the research and development work on this class of vessels, a USN officer was given the task of researching worldwide experience in defence from attacks by anti-ship missiles. Like so many other US military officers in similar positions, he was sent to Israel with the task of working himself through the local military archives. In turn, the Israelis provided him with what they described as, 'precise details of Iraqi combat experiences', stressing these included exactly *50 combat firings* of AM.39 Exocet anti-ship missiles. Rather surprised by this figure, and as somebody considering it 'well-known' that the Iraqis had fired about 10 times as many Exocets in combat against Iran, co-author Cooper was naïve enough to challenge the content of the Israeli reports. What came in response was a statement to the effect of, 'They are Israelis and my friends. I stand by my conclusions and data'. From that moment onwards, it was clear: there is an urgent need to research about the air-naval warfare between Iran and Iraq, otherwise this aspect of that conflict was certain to remain entirely unknown.

The book presented here is far from perfect, and well short of providing any 'final truth': because not only documentation about the Iranian military build-up of the 1970s, but especially the Iraqi wartime documentation remain beyond reach, much of the story about naval warfare during this conflict is yet to be told. *Iran-Iraq Naval War* is thus unlikely to offer precise answers to all the questions, and certain to contain a number of mistakes. However, this is unlikely to change any time soon: indeed, our hope is that its publication might encourage additional interest and research into the naval warfare between Iran and Iraq: the longest and most intensive war of this kind in decades.

1

SETTING THE SCENE

Known as the 'Sea above Akkad' by the Babylonians, or the 'Bitter Sea' by the Assyrians, the 'Gulf of Fars', or by modern-day Arabs as al-Khalij al-Arabi – the 'Arabian Gulf' – what has been known as the Persian Gulf since ancient Greek times is a waterway defined by the International Hydrographic Organisation as running from two capes: Ras al-Kuh in Iran, at 25°48'N, to Ras Limah in Saudi Arabia, at 25°57'N. It is 533 nautical miles (989 kilometres) long while the width varies from 30nm (56km) at the Straits of Hormuz to 180nm (340km) at the widest point, and the depth is between 25 and 100 metres. Overall, the Persian Gulf has a surface of about 251,000 square kilometres. While it appears a wide body of water, a combination of coral reefs along many coasts, numerous islands, shoals, and gas- and oil-exploitation platforms, severely restrict the deep-draft traffic to a few well-charted passages. Because of this, to modern-day seafarers, 'the Gulf' appears as a long and narrow 'canyon'. The air above it is clouded into an almost continuous haze of damp and dust so even on the clearest day visibility is reduced to just 3–5nm: the summer monsoon starts in early April and reduces visibility sometimes to less than a nautical mile while sand and fine dust in a damp, hot, wind can damage sensitive electronics.

Historically, the Persian Gulf was dominated by the succession of Achaemenid and then the Persian empires for thousands of years, and also after that country was renamed the Empire of Iran in 1935. Persian merchants and naval forces always maintained a strong maritime presence, and were in control of not only most of the islands, or had major naval bases in what are nowadays Bahrain and Oman, but also ranged up and down the rivers of the empire north of it, including the Shatt al-Arab (or 'Arvand Rood' in Farsi) and Tigris in modern-day Iraq, all the way to the Nile in Egypt, and Sind in India. After the fall of the Achaemenid Empire, the Sassanid Empire ruled the northern half and, from time to time, parts of the southern half of the Persian Gulf, which became as important as the Silk Road.

At the beginning of the sixteenth century, the Portuguese appeared on the scene. In 1521, their force led by Antonio Correia invaded Persian-controlled Bahrain and assumed control over the wealthy pearl industry. They were expelled by the Persian Emperor Shah Abbas on 29 April 1602, and this day has been commemorated as the National Persian Gulf Day in Iran ever since. With English help, Abbas then liberated the port of Bandar in 1615, and named the town after himself. Five years later, he also secured Hormuz Island from the Portuguese, but then opened a flourishing commerce with the Portuguese, and Dutch, French, Spanish and English merchants, all of whom were granted privileges.

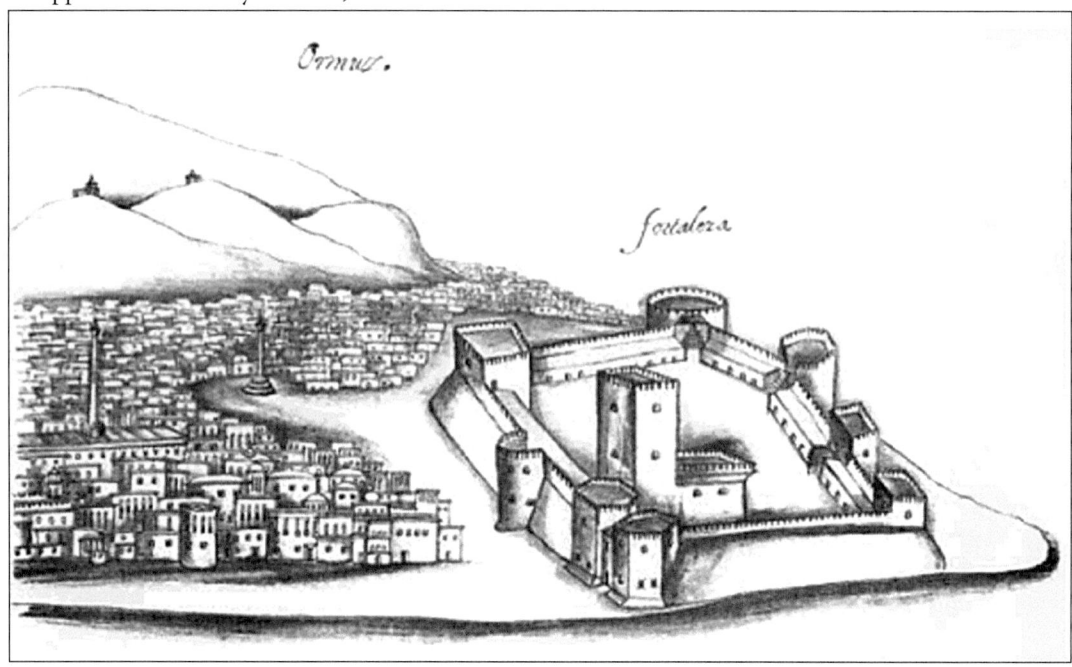

A Portuguese castle on Hormuz Island, from the seventeenth century. (Joao Dos Santos de Sousa Campos, *Arquitectura Militar Portuguesa no Golfe Persico-Ormuz, Keshm e Larak*, Coimbra, 2008)

A T-26 light tank of the 6th Tank Division, Soviet Army, on a street in Tabriz, north-western Iran, in 1941. (Russian MOD)

A British map from 1747 of the Persian Empire, showing the Persian Gulf. (Bowen, *A Complete System of Geography*)

THE COURSE OF RESOURCES

The Empire of Great Britain established itself in various degrees of control over the western side of the Persian Gulf, starting from 1763, but especially after the Persian Gulf campaign against the piracy of the al-Qassimi tribe. Starting from 1871, the Ottoman Empire attempted – but never managed – to assert itself in control over the northern and eastern coasts, although the at-Thani tribe of Qatar peacefully submitted itself to their rule. In turn, the British forced the Ottomans to completely withdraw from the area during the First World War, in the course of the Mesopotamia Campaign of 1915–18. In addition to traditional commerce, pearls, fishery, and the strategic position, it was the discovery of massive oil reserves in the Masjed Suleiman area of western Persia, by an Admiralty-funded British expedition in May 1908, that prompted many in London to consider the Persian Gulf to be one of the most significant waterways in the world. Less than a year later, after securing concessions for extracting, refining and export, the British established the Anglo-Persian Oil Company (later the Anglo-Iranian Oil Company, AIOC), and then connected the newly discovered oilfields with a 217-kilometre-long pipeline to the previously isolated and sparsely populated Abadan Island on the Shatt al-Arab, where the AIOC constructed the largest oil refinery in the world. By 1913, the infrastructure was expanded through another tanker-loading terminal, constructed in the port of Bandar-e Mahshahr, about 100km east of Abadan. Persia thus became the first country in the Middle East to export commercially viable petroleum resources.

The next important point in time occurred in 1925, when, after years of war, turmoil, and foreign interventions, Reza Khan – a military officer, then minister of war and prime minister of the Persian Empire – established himself in power in Tehran and crowned himself as Reza Shah Pahlavi. He launched a major land reform, built infrastructure and schools, modernised cities, and initiated a massive expansion of transportation networks. Reza Shah's principal project was the construction of the Trans-Iranian Railway, initiated in 1927. Entirely completed with the help of indigenous capital in 1938, this linked the port of Bandar Shahpur (present day Bandar-e Khomeini; and known colloquially as 'BIK' to Iranian sailors) in the Persian Gulf, via Ahwaz and Qom, to the port of Bandar Shah (nowadays Bandar Torkaman) on the Caspian Sea. In early 1940, the British – purportedly concerned about growing German influence in Iraq and Iran – began accusing Iran of supporting Nazism and being 'pro-German'. Actually, Reza Shah declared neutrality, but London feared about the security of the huge Abadan refinery and its oil production that reached about 10.2 million metric tons a year. Combined with the existence of the Trans-Iranian Railway, this was one of the principal reasons for the decisions of the governments of Great Britain and the Union of Soviet Socialist Republics (USSR; colloquially 'Soviet Union') to invade the Empire of Iran in 1941, and thus secure the so-called 'Persian Corridor': a critical path along which the Allies transported military and industrial supplies to help the USSR fight the Nazi invasion.

OIL – EVERYWHERE

Meanwhile, in 1912, the Ottoman Empire had granted a concession for oil exploration to the British-controlled Turkish Petroleum Company (TPC). Entirely unsuccessful at first, and then disrupted by the First World War, the TPC remained operational: it was brought under the control of a consortium of British, British-Dutch, French, and US corporations and renamed the Iraqi Petroleum Company (IPC). In 1925, the IPC obtained a 75-year concession to search for oil north of Kirkuk. This time, it was highly successfully: in 1927, it discovered an extensive underground oilfield in the Kirkuk area and, four years later, obtained a 75-year permission for its exploitation in exchange for minimal royalties and the construction of two pipelines to the Mediterranean Sea. The British insisted on this pipeline ending at a terminal in Haifa, in the British Mandate of Palestine, while the French wanted a pipeline to the terminal in Tripoli, in French-controlled Lebanon. Correspondingly, starting in the Kirkuk area, the IPC constructed a pipeline in Y-form. This was largely completed by 1935, but – primarily because the British were well-supplied with oil from the USA and Persia, and, after the fall of France, in 1940, blocked the fork to Tripoli – no significant amounts of Iraqi crude were exported before the late 1940s, when additional oil resources were discovered in southern Iraq. This finding resulted in the search for a new export venue. In the 1950s, the first oil-loading terminal was constructed at the south-eastern-most edge of Iraqi territorial waters, south-east of al-Faw, though as a part of the al-Basra Oil Terminal: Mina Khowr al-Amiyah (KAAOT). By 1974, the second such facility was constructed by Brown & Root, the Mina al-Bakr (ABOT). Both were connected by pipelines to oilfields west of Basra.

Contrary to the situation in Iraq where the primary British interest seems to have been the prevention of other powers assuming control over local oil-sources, when oil was discovered in the centre of the island of Bahrain in 1932, exports began two years later. Meanwhile, oil was discovered in northern and southern Kuwait – the economy of which was completely ruined during the First World War – and, in 1934, the local ruler Sheikh Ahmed al-Jaber as-Sabah granted the first oil concession to the Kuwait Oil Company, jointly owned by APOC, and the Gulf Oil Corporation from the USA. Further discoveries of crude and steadily rising exports boosted and revolutionised the sheikhdom's economy, making it vital to British strategic interests: securing them was a co-reason for the British invasions of Iran and Iraq in 1941.

Reza Shah Pahlavi (centre), and his son Mohammed Reza (right), inspecting a warship of the Imperial Iranian Navy before the Anglo-Soviet invasion of 1941. (Leon Manoucherians collection)

Two Royal Navy cruisers moored in the Abadan area during the Second World War. (Leon Manoucherians collection)

THE IRAN CRISIS OF 1946

The British and the Soviets forced Reza Shah to abdicate and installed his son, Crown Prince Mohammed Reza Pahlavi in nominal power, though in reality they kept Iran under military occupation under promise to withdraw within six months after the cessation of hostilities against Nazi Germany and its allies. The agreement was of particular importance not only because of the Persian Corridor, but also because of the type of fuels produced in Iran. The Abadan refinery was primarily designed to supply the Royal Navy with heavy oil. However, by the early 1940s it became the only refinery outside the Gulf of Mexico and east of Suez producing 100-octane aviation fuel: its importance for the Allied war effort in the Pacific in particular was crucial. Unsurprisingly, the British took extensive care to secure the centre and the south of the country, and to carefully guard all the oil manufacturing facilities in the country; about 30,000 military personnel from the USA deployed to maintain the Persian Corridor and to train the re-established and re-formed Iranian armed forces.

The occupation caused deep resentment among Iranians, and the government in Tehran took great care to effect a British withdrawal as promised. However, in early 1946, the Soviets – who controlled the north of the country, refused to withdraw. Instead, they attempted to create two Moscow-sponsored para-states of ethnic Azeris and Kurds in north-western Iran. The resulting war between the Iranian forces and Soviet-supported Azerbaijani and Kurdish forces resulted in over 2,000 casualties. Eventually, only negotiations by Iranian prime minister Ahmad Qavam and severe diplomatic pressure from the USA prompted the Soviets to withdraw, thus ending one of the early crises of what became known as the Cold War.

COLD WAR

While the British attempted to return to 'business as usual' after the Second World War – mainly through securing their positions in Iran, Iraq, and Kuwait – the now dominating superpower of the USA became obsessed with confronting the USSR. The early phase of the related American activities was characterised by a two-fold strategy: officially, Washington was striving to create military alliances among states bordering the USSR, with the aim of 'stopping the spread of Communism'. Unofficially, and always under the pretext of 'countering the Communist threat', the Central Intelligence Agency (CIA) of the USA became involved in suppressing any kind of nationalist- or other type of local movement that threatened Western dominance, no matter where. Perhaps the most dramatic demonstration of such behaviour occurred in Iran in 1951–53. The government of the Iranian prime minister Mohammed Mossadegh attempted to merely verify that the AIOC was paying the contracted royalties. The British refused, prompting the Majlis – the parliament of Iran – to nationalise all of the oil industry in Iran and to expel foreign corporate representatives from the country. In revenge, London not only instigated a worldwide boycott of Iranian oil, almost bankrupting the government in Tehran, but also deployed its armed forces to seize the Abadan oil refinery and began plotting to topple Mossadegh. This decision was supported by the administration of the US President Dwight D. Eisenhower and by Iranians who argued that the country lacked skilled managerial and technical staff to exploit and sell its oil on its own. Eventually, the CIA organised a coup, and Mossadegh's replacement by a government under General Fazlollah Zahedi, which in turn allowed Mohammed Reza Pahlavi to rule as a monarch – although heavily reliant on the US support to hold on to power. Iranian oil exports, which came to a standstill in 1953, recovered only very slowly: in 1954, the NIOC was thus forced to enter a new agreement with a consortium of international companies, comprising the AIOC – reorganised as British Petroleum (BP) – and Royal Dutch Shell, along with several American cartels that made sure British dominance was avoided.

The US influence grew even further when, in the same year, Washington's pressure and promises of military and economic aid effected the creation of the Middle East Treaty Organization (colloquially the 'Baghdad Pact'; renamed the Central Treaty Organization, CENTO, in 1959). The pact initially included Iran, Iraq, Pakistan, Turkey, and the UK. However, it never managed to attract the dominating Arab power of the time and the future Arab superpower – the Republic of Egypt and the Kingdom of Saudi Arabia, respectively – as members. Moreover, Iraq left the alliance after the anti-monarchist and anti-British Tammuz Revolution of 1958, while Kuwait remained a British protectorate until 1961, and never joined CENTO.

Despite the partial failure of CENTO, the USA did manage to secure their influence in the Empire of Iran and the Kingdom of Saudi Arabia. In turn, Great Britain was reduced to maintaining the security of Kuwait and a number of so-called 'trucial states' along the western and southern side of the Persian Gulf: by the time of the general British withdrawal from the area in 1971, these were organised into the Kingdom of Bahrain, the State of Qatar, the United Arab Emirates, and the Sultanate of Oman.[1]

YET MORE OIL…

During the late 1940s and early 1950s, multiple US oil companies made ever bigger discoveries of oil and gas deposits around and in the Persian Gulf. Exports from Saudi Arabia had commenced in 1939 but were deeply overshadowed by discoveries in the early 1950s, including a huge oilfield north-east of Ras as-Saffaniyah; another one – Manifa – south-east of the same town; one in the Jubali area, and no fewer than three in the Dhahran area. By 1962, oil exports commenced from the Umm Sahif field, 110km north-west of Abu Dhabi, thus converting the future United Arab Emirates into another oil-rich nation, almost overnight, and this was followed by discoveries of oil in south-western Qatar. By 1970, the Iranians had also discovered huge oil deposits under the the Persian Gulf: at first about 40km west of Khark, and then further south-west. As a result, other companies and countries arrived at similar ideas, resulting in – amongst others – discoveries of a giant oilfield in the northern central Persian Gulf (Esfandiar), the biggest gas field stretching from the northern shores of Qatar almost to Farsi Island (South Pars, known as the North Field in Qatar), and a large number of smaller oil and gas fields in the southern Persian Gulf, stretching from the eastern verge of Qatari territorial waters, all the way to the Hormuz Straits. Unsurprisingly, by the mid-1970s, the Gulf was full of offshore drilling- and oil/gas-exploitation rigs, and about two dozen undersea pipelines were in operation.

Therefore, the oil production and exports of Iran, Iraq, Saudi Arabia and other countries in the Persian Gulf were increasing at a terrific rate – even more so as the industrialised West continued increasing its dependence on the seas for the transit of raw materials, prompting all oil exporters to further intensify exploration of new oilfields and the expansion of their oil industries. In Iran, for example, the Abadan refinery had proved unable to cope with the growing demand during the Second World War. Moreover, its loading terminal in Bandar-e Mahshahr could not keep up with the rapidly growing size of tanker ships. A deep-water oil export terminal was necessary – and eventually found on Khark Island, in the northern Persian Gulf, off the coast of Bushehr. This resulted in

MERCHANT SHIP REVOLUTION

Meanwhile, the mercantile marines of the 1950s experienced an outright revolution, which was comparable to that of steam replacing sail in the 1880s. As of the late 1930s and early 1940s, the world's mercantile fleets were dominated by those of the imperial powers, and especially Great Britain, and most hulls were laid down in European yards while crews were drawn from domestic sources. Almost every ship, even the great passenger liners, carried freight which was loaded piecemeal into the holds. The freighter – nowadays called the General Dry Cargo Carrier (GDC) – was the most common merchant vessel. Typical GDCs displaced between 5,000 and 10,000 gross registered tons (grt) and were powered by labour-intensive steam turbines fired by fuel oil. Despite the brief upsurge in the US merchant marine, little changed until after the end of the Second World War: American yards had constructed hundreds of 'Liberty ship' merchantmen, including the VC2-S-AP1 or 'Victory ship': a freighter of 7,200grt (or 10,600 deadweight tonnage – dwt). Tankers were of similar size: average hulls of the early 1940s displaced 15,000grt, and they were supplanted by the wartime T2 tanker design, which displaced 9,900dwt or 15,850dwt. Although a few tankers had diesel engines, most were powered by steam.

As the colonial empires began to dissolve through the 1950s, their navies were replaced by those of newly independent states which, together with those of Japan and China, then proved more competitive than their previous masters. Moreover, this competitiveness extended into south-eastern Europe, where Greece, Turkey, and Soviet-allied countries of the Warsaw Pact proved capable of offering their service at attractive prices. Certainly enough, shipping ownership remained strong in Europe (together with the insurance and chartering businesses); however, aiming to reduce their costs, European shipowners began registering their vessels under flags of convenience, especially Liberia and Panama. Not only did this provide financial and law enforcement incentives but also meant they did not have to man vessels with increasingly expensive domestic crews. Ever more Asian officers and men were brought in, with the added benefit that they lacked strong trades unions who would seek better pay and conditions. With neither Liberia nor Panama possessing any naval presence, merchant ships were deprived of protection but with no apparent threats, shipowners were willing to accept the risk.

As a result, the British merchant marine decreased dramatically. In 1976, it was the third largest merchant fleet with a total of 31,923,000grt. As soon thereafter as 1980, it was down to the fourth place, with 27,135,000grt. By 1983, it was seventh with only 19,121,000grt. Not only the total capacity and displacement, but the number of ships operated by the British decreased dramatically too; from 1,378 vessels with 51,661,000dwt in the Third Quarter of 1978 to 504 with 10,621,000dwt in the First Quarter of 1987; the bulk-carrier and tanker fleets dropped by 59 percent and 72 percent during the same period, respectively. In comparison, by New Year's Day 1987, Liberian-flagged ships totalled 98,502,000dwt (or 16 percent of the market) while Panama officially 67,444,000dwt (or 11 percent of the market). The third biggest merchant navy of the 1970s and 1980s was that of Japan, with 55,488,000dwt (or 9 percent). The British was down to 12,539,000dwt (or 2 percent).[3]

While the new nations' merchant fleets benefitted from lower costs, their success reflected the fact that owners were more willing to exploit advances in naval architecture such as welding rather

The container ship *Kowloon Bay* underway with a cargo of containers in the early 1970s. The introduction of containers prompted the computerisation of loading and unloading, ensuring that they were stowed on board in the correct order of their unloading, greatly reducing the time necessary for this process. (Tom Cooper collection)

than riveting hulls. Most of these advances were made by Far Eastern yards, notably Japan, which not only had lower costs but also were willing to innovate, unlike the European yards where even the most innovative shipbuilders – such as in Germany – were rapidly outpaced. Simultaneously, propulsion moved from steam turbine to marine diesel and even gas turbine, all of which were more efficient in terms of performance and cost, as the engine rooms required fewer men thanks to the new technology and electronic controls.

In a world increasingly dependent upon oil, this revolution in ship design was led by tankers – and wars: in 1956, the Suez Canal was closed because of the Anglo-French and Israeli aggressions on Egypt. Therefore, tankers had to sail around the Cape of Good Hope. This acted as a catalyst for owners who began realising that larger ships meant more efficient transport: this conclusion led to the emergence of so-called 'supertankers'. As of 1955, the largest was the British-built, Greek-owned *Spyros Niarchos* with 30,708grt or 47,500dwt. Within only three years, this was surpassed by the Japanese-constructed but US-owned *Universe Apollo* of 72,132grt or 104,520dwt. While the war of 1956 resulted in only a temporary closure of the Suez Canal, the June 1967 Arab-Israeli War caused a closure of the vital waterway that lasted for years, and led to a rapid and massive growth in the size of tankers, which reached such proportions that entirely new terminology had to be developed to describe them properly:

- Very Large Crude Carrier (VLCC) could be up to 400 metres long and carry 250,000dwt, while the
- Ultra Large Crude Carrier (ULCC) could be more than 415 metres long with a capacity of up to 500,000dwt

The pace of this change is best gauged by the fact that *Universe Apollo* was scrapped in 1979, by when the world's largest supertanker was the Japanese-constructed and Hong Kong-owned ULCC *Seawise Giant* of 238,558grt or 564,763dwt.

Parallel with the emergence of colossal tanker ships there was a revolution in the movement of dry cargo. The traditional piecemeal loading and unloading was slow and vulnerable to breakage and pilfering. Unsurprisingly, in the 1920s the idea emerged of carrying cargo in containers. Container transport came into wider use in the early 1950s, but it was only in 1955 that the standardised, 13ft-long steel container with a twistlock mechanism at each corner (for easier loading and unloading) appeared. By the end of the same year, the first purpose-built container ship had carried 600 of them from Vancouver, British Columbia, to Skagway in Alaska. The advantages of containers and container ships were rapidly appreciated and five international standard-length containers ranging in length from 6.10 to 16.15 metres were developed with capacity expressed as 20-foot Equivalent Units (TEU) – which is 22 to 27 tonnes. The principal advantage of containers was experienced by both wharf- and shipowners: wharfs required fewer dockers, while shipowners could precisely calculate how long it would take to unload and re-load their vessels. The success of the concept may be gauged from the decline of the general dry cargo ships: these carried 32 million tonnes of freight in 1982, 23.2 million tonnes in 1984 and in 1986 fewer than 18 million tonnes.[4]

At one point in time, container transport reached such popularity that the idea emerged to let trucks and trains drive – or roll – onto, and off vessels, rather than being offloaded. Thus came into being the term 'roll-on, roll-off' – or Ro-Ro – ships. Arguably, a similar concept was used extensively for railways from 1850, but after the Second World War landing craft were used for cross-Channel operations only: a few dedicated Ro-Ros were then developed as ferries in the USA in the 1960s. Eventually, it was car manufacturers that made the most of Ro-Ros in order to transport large numbers of vehicles at once. In addition to their economy of operation, supertankers, container ships and Ro-Ros offered another advantage: they were all huge, and had a very robust structure including thick steel plates, which in turn meant that they were very difficult to sink.

At 484,000dwt, the ULCC *Globtik Tokyo* was the largest oil tanker in the world during the early 1970s. Construction of such ships was made necessary by the closure of the Suez Canal after the June 1967 Arab-Israeli War. (Tom Cooper collection)

An aerial view of the port of Khorramshahr, on the Shatt al-Arab, with a row of ships (including at least four 'Liberty ships' constructed during the Second World War). Despite the construction of numerous much larger facilities, Khorramshahr lost only a little of its importance up to September 1980. (Leon Manoucherians collection)

was expanded into the major general port of the northern Persian Gulf. It had a total of 40 berths for general cargo, containers, grain silos, barges, and iron ore, and warehouses and open storage areas with a total capability of 171,000 square metres and 10,900,000 square kilometres, respectively. The 42-mile-long (78km) channel connecting Bandar-e-Shahpour with the Persian Gulf – the Khowr al-Moussa – was dredged to a depth of 25m, enabling the operation of the biggest merchant ships available at the time.

In addition to Bushehr opposite to Khark, further down the coast was Bandar-e Abbas, near the Straits of Hormuz: there, the old port (present day Bandar-e Bahonar) was converted into a naval base, while a new commercial port with six jetties for cargo ships and two for tankers was constructed nearby. This was soon concluded to be insufficient, and an Italian company was contracted to build an even larger port named Aryamehr (present day Port Shahid Rajaei). This had an entrance canal 14m deep, with three basins and 35 jetties for ships up to 40,000 tonnes – for general cargo, bulk cargo, and containers, and three jetties for tankers. Arguably, all the work in question was incomplete even as of 1979, but unloading with the help of barges became possible. Finally, during the second half of the 1970s, the Iranians began developing an immense project worth a total of US$8 billion for construction of a large port in the Bay of Chabahar (formerly Bandar-e Beheshti), on Iran's coast on the Indian Ocean. This was to receive a huge air base, major naval facility, and a deep-water port by 1984. Despite an investment of $350 million, Chabahar was never completed and never became capable of supporting naval operations; just four berths in Port Shahid Beheshti, on the eastern side, and a portion of the nearby air base, on the western side, were completed. Nevertheless, the bay continued providing an excellent anchorage for merchants. Overall, by 1976, the unloading capacity of the Iranian ports reached 12,000,000 tonnes and there were no unloading delays, contrary to earlier times, when these plagued the country's facilities.[2]

the construction of the famous 'Y-pipeline' connecting Abadan with the largest ever oil hub, in the early 1960s. The nearby general port of Bushehr was also expanded at the same time. Such works were also of increasing importance because constantly growing exports of petrochemical products resulted in constantly growing income of the exporting countries: with these lacking their own industries to produce consumer goods, they had to import most consumables such as cars and electronics. This meant a constantly growing amount of trade and naval traffic. Almost all of the existing ports in the Persian Gulf were significantly expanded in the 1960s and 1970s, and a number of new facilities constructed. The most important Iranian port remained that of Khorramshahr, which even as of the mid-1970s still handled 65 percent of the dry cargo imports of Iran. However, the most fascinating and rapid growth was experienced by the port of Bandar-e Shahpour. Situated only about a dozen kilometres east of Bandar-e Mahshahr, it was once a desolate place situated near the terminus of the Trans-Iranian Railway. During the Second World War, the US armed forces constructed a single jetty and two shipping berths as the starting point of the Persian Corridor. However, that was diminutive in comparison to the explosive development of this port during the 1970s, when Bandar-e Shahpour

BRITISH WITHDRAWAL

The modern-day organisation of the maritime traffic in and out of the Persian Gulf developed as a result of several factors, including the local geography and above-mentioned developments of the 1960s

Table 1: US and Soviet ship days in the Indian Ocean (Surface combatants and Auxiliaries)[8]

Year	1968	1969	1970	1971	1972	1973
US Navy	1,688	1,315	1,246	1,337	1,435	2,154
Soviet	1,760	3,668	3,579	3,804	8,007	8,543

and 1970s. Early during this period, the area was still dominated by the British presence, even if this was – usually – rather 'token' and based upon the deployment of a few frigates and amphibious warfare ships of the Royal Navy in ports like Aden in Yemen, or Manama in Bahrain. Occasionally, the French Navy (*Marine nationale*) would mark its presence by deploying warships operated from the island of La Réunion, between Madagascar and Mauritius, in the Indian Ocean. The US military presence grew only slowly. In August 1949, the US Navy (USN) established its Middle East Force, based in Manama, while the US Air Force (USAF) profited from Saudi permission to use the Dhahran Air Base (AB). However, for most of the 1950s and 1960s, the US military presence was limited to occasional passages or courtesy visits by larger vessels.[5]

This situation began to change towards the end of the 'Swinging Sixties'. During a period of major economic problems, in January 1968 Great Britain announced the end of its century-old military presence 'east of Suez' by 1971. Taking place around the same time, the physical and psychological consequences of the Vietnam War made the Americans reluctant to accept additional commitment of their armed forces abroad. This undermined all the existing Western defence concepts for the Middle East, and was of particular importance for all the Arab countries along the western and southern side of the Persian Gulf, granted independence from Britain between 1961 and 1971: all of these had only small populations and – except for Kuwait – underdeveloped economies and almost non-existent armed forces.[6]

Around the same time, the Western powers noticed the increased presence of Soviet warships in the region. Arguably, Russian warships had regularly transferred from their bases in western Russia to the Pacific via the Indian Ocean since the times of the Russo-Japanese War of 1904–05; Soviet warships followed a similar route since 1939. However, during the 1960s, civilian ships of the Soviet space research organisation became an almost permanent presence, and from 1965 Moscow's influence grew through diplomatic support for New Delhi in the Indo-Pakistani conflict. During the following years, the USSR exported a number of warships to India, and deployed a small detachment of Projeckt 641-class (ASCC/NATO codename 'Foxtrot') diesel-electric submarines, supported by supply ships in the Indian Ocean. In August 1968, the Pacific Fleet of the Soviet armed forces established its 8th Squadron, responsible for maintaining a permanent presence through the regular rotation of destroyers and frigates, submarines, minesweepers, and amphibious assault vessels in the Indian Ocean. Indeed, by 1971, this group was dubbed the Soviet Indian Ocean Squadron, and bolstered to two cruisers, two destroyers, seven submarines, at least one intelligence-gathering ship, four space and research ships, and nine support vessels.[7] Over the following years, the Soviets established a near-permanent presence in the People's Democratic Republic of Yemen (South Yemen, which included the former British Protectorate of Aden)

OUTSOURCING DEFENCE: THE NIXON DOCTRINE

The burden of fighting a prolonged war and negative experience from the conflict in Southeast Asia eventually prompted the administration of President Nixon into a decision that US allies should bear greater responsibility for their own defence. Thus came into being the Nixon Doctrine, under which, instead of deploying US troops to ensure the safety of its allies, the USA would help them build-up their own armed forces through sales of equipment and the provision of training.

With the imminent departure of Great Britain, this meant that the Americans were on the hunt for a 'new major ally' in the Middle East. Available options were the Empire of Iran and the Kingdom of Saudi Arabia, which Washington believed could balance each other – although the population of the latter was only a fraction of that of the former. Mohammed Reza Shah Pahlavi proved happy to accept his new role as protector of the Persian Gulf and the Middle East, which he considered part of the tradition of his country, and for Washington's acceptance of an existing regional reality. In fact, Nixon's decision not only reversed a quarter-century-old policy of regarding a massive military build-up of any state in the region as destabilising, but it also complicated efforts to establish a smooth relationship between Iran and Saudi Arabia – even more so because the latter viewed not only Iran, but also Iraq as a menace. Moreover, Washington was always concerned about the Shah's reliability, and the stability of his regime – and they were not alone in this: during Anglo-American talks of October 1974, a British official and expert on the Middle East warned his US counterparts to watch out because the Shah might overreach himself.[9]

Another issue constantly troubling the US influence in the Middle East was the Arab-Israeli conflict, which culminated in the October 1973 War between an alliance of Arab states led by Egypt and Syria, and Israel. During this conflict, Bahrain formally banned USN warships from using its ports, while Iran provided diplomatic support to the Arabs, even if clandestinely providing ammunition and supplies to Israel. Although both Bahrain and the USA tacitly ignored the ban, already alerted by the growing presence of Soviet warships, the Americans became concerned enough to start considering a permanent military presence in the Indian Ocean. As a result, Washington and London reached an agreement about an atoll in the British Indian Ocean Territory near the Seychelles: Diego Garcia. In June 1968, the US Congress granted funding for the construction of a US Navy communication facility and improvement of the local airfield, while the British evicted the 900 inhabitants.[10] In March 1971, the US armed forces then initiated work on constructing a major base, capable of supporting Boeing B-52 Stratofortress heavy bombers, and a port capable of receiving the largest warships of the USN, together with extensive storage facilities.

Ironically, the new US base at Diego Garcia was still very much in the future: indeed, it appeared 'too little, too late' to men like the Shah of Iran. Concerned about the growing Soviet presence and convinced that Washington was unable to organise any significant naval presence, he flexed his muscles before the British had completed their withdrawal. He made no secret of his intention to recover the Tunb Islands (Tonb-e Bozorg and Tonb-e Kuchak in Farsi, and Tunb el-Kubra and Tunb el-Sughra in Arabic), and Abu Musa in the lower Persian Gulf – traditionally controlled by Persia, but illegally seized by the Sheikh of Sharjah in 1904, and 'assigned' by London to the future United Arab Emirates. However, in exchange for Tehran abandoning its long-standing claim to Bahrain, London then advised the British Ambassador to Iran to inform the Shah of the exact time the British would withdraw from the Persian Gulf: at 22.00hrs on 30 November 1971, the night the last British troops were to withdraw, the ambassador relayed this information to the Iranian government, enabling Iranian Marines – supported by the IIN and the USN – to quickly secure both the Tunb Islands and Abu Musa as the last tweak of the lion's tail.

LOCAL MERCHANT FLEETS AND MARITIME TRAFFIC IN AND OUT OF THE PERSIAN GULF

As of the 1950s, the mass of the cargo transiting the Straits of Hormuz and the Persian Gulf was carried by foreign vessels. However, in 1961, Iran began the work on creation of a national shipping line. This came into being in August 1967, as Arya Shipping Lines. Initially, it was a modest service with only six vessels – including two coasters – but by the mid-1970s it had expanded to 42 hulls with a total capacity of 525,000 dwt. Further increased through the acquisition of smaller tankers by the National Iranian Tanker Company (NITC) – a list of which is provided in Table 2 – the expansion continued from 135 hulls (479,718grt) in 1976 to 208 hulls (1,194,675grt) in 1980. In similar fashion, Iraq's merchant fleet grew from almost zero in the 1940s to 56 hulls with 310,594grt in the early 1970s, and then to 123 vessels (with 1,328,256grt) in 1976. Contrary to what might be expected, it comprised only 20 tankers: there were 28 freighters, two container ships, two ferries, and a refrigerated cargo ship, with a total capacity of 2,559,835dwt.[11]

Together with constantly – and rapidly – growing volumes of maritime traffic, these were the factors that resulted in both the political and nautical maps of the Persian Gulf of the 1970s (and still valid today, despite the continued dispute over the Tunb Islands and Abu Musa). Its northern and eastern coasts remained dominated by Iran: The western and south-western sides of the Persian Gulf are dominated by the Kingdom of Saudi Arabia (with a coastline of around 1,300 kilometres). At the head lies the Republic of Iraq, with a coastline of 31nm (58km), while from the north towards the south along the southern side are the State of Kuwait (with 270nm/499km), Kingdom of Bahrain (87nm/161km), the State of Qatar (with 30nm/56km), the United Arab Emirates (485nm/900km), and the Sultanate of Oman (54nm/100km). Indeed, Oman shares control of the Gulf's entrance through the Straits of Hormuz with Iran. However, most of the waterway is within Iranian territorial waters because it is there that the water is deep enough for big ships, because Iran's northern coast extends along it, and Iran controls the Tunb Islands at the northern entrance.

In the light of constantly growing maritime traffic in and out of the Persian Gulf, during the 1960s the International Maritime Organisation arranged the flow of shipping through the Hormuz Straits in the form of 'recommendations': none of these was mandatory, but they were respected by almost everybody. The Hormuz Strait is shallowest towards the north: its greatest depth – 214 metres – is at a point between the Iranian coast in the north and Didamar or Little Quoin Island, and Cape Musandam in Oman, 48.5nm (90km) to the south. It has a tidal range of 2.13 metres and the surface current is four knots (7.4km/h). It is divided into five zones:

- Along the Iranian and Omani coasts, there are 5–6nm wide channels for coastal traffic.
- The Northern Zone is a 7–8nm wide channel for tankers loaded with crude oil, gas, or other petrochemical products, leaving the Gulf.

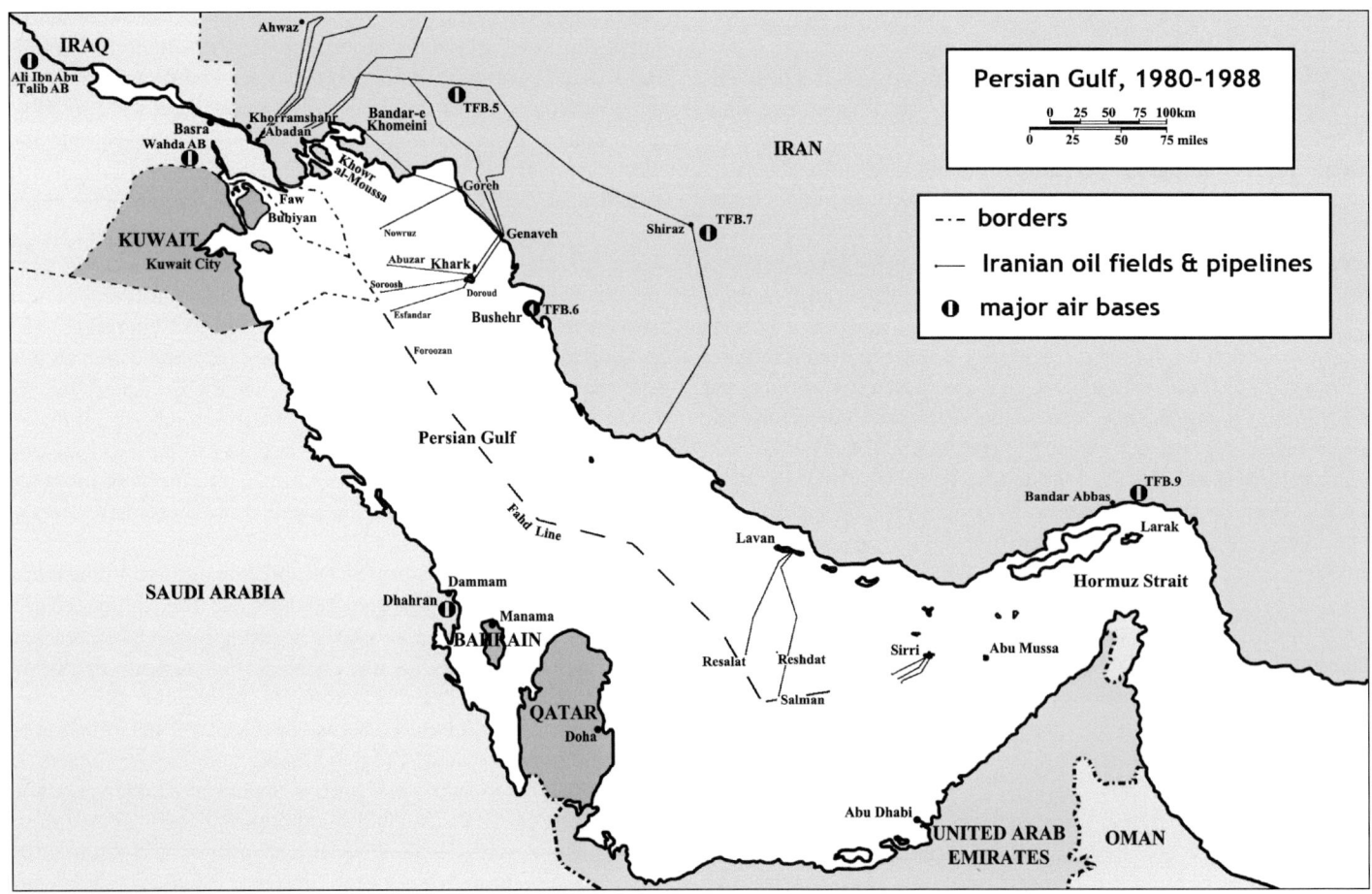

(Map by Tom Cooper)

- The Central is a 2–3nm wide channel connecting the Northern Zone with the Southern Zone.
- Southern Zone is a 7–8nm wide channel for tankers travelling in ballast (i.e. empty, but loading water for their better seakeeping performance).

Table 2: NITC Tanker Fleet (Product Carriers), 1980		
Name	Year built	Dwt
Minab-5	1971	29,684
Iran Gas	1972	11,000
Azna	1973	25,558
Mokran	1973	26,651
Marun	1973	25,651
Minab-2	1973	25,530
Minab-3	1973	25,650
Minab-4	1973	25,650
Shirvan	1979	69,360
Tabriz	1980	69,498
Total tonnage: 333,232		

SHATT AL-ARAB

While the majority of the borders between states with access to the Persian Gulf are widely accepted, there was one point that became a cause for fierce dispute between Iran and Iraq: the Shatt al-Arab. This waterway is the estuary of the Tigris and Euphrates Rivers. In 1937, it was defined by the Saadabad Treaty as the border between Iran and Iraq – with one important rule: in its southern sector, the border was identified as lying at the low-water mark of the eastern, that is Iranian, shore. Correspondingly, not only was the Shatt almost entirely inside Iraq, but ships underway to Abadan and the – ever busier – nearby Khorramshahr, had to travel through Iraqi territorial waters on the way to their destination, and again on the way out. As might have been expected, as Iran grew powerful in the 1960s, Tehran began challenging this portion of the treaty and demanded that the border should be revised in accordance with the international custom: to run at the thalweg – essentially the middle point – of the waterway. Iraq resisted and demanded that all foreign ships moving up and down the Shatt al-Arab fly its flag. The crisis reached its culminating point during the Second Iraqi-Kurdish War of 1974–75, when Iran began supporting the Kurdish insurgency in northern Iraq, which managed to fight the Iraqi counteroffensives to a standstill. The war was still going on when, as a result of secret negotiations between Baghdad and Tehran, the Algiers Accord was announced on 6 March 1975. In this document, Iraq officially accepted Iran's claim that the thalweg should form the common border in the Shatt al-Arab, thereby allowing for Iranian navigation of the Shatt al-Arab. In exchange, Iran promptly ceased supporting the Kurdish insurgency and withdrew all of its troops from Iraqi territory. However, the leadership in Iraq – correctly – felt forced into this concession, and deeply resented Iran's taking advantage of its superior military position.[12]

2
THE MOTHER OF MILITARY BUILD-UPS

Parallel with assuming the British role of the guarantor of security of the Persian Gulf, and bolstered by constantly increasing oil revenues and the Nixon Doctrine, the Shah of Iran began an unprecedented military build-up – and announced in public that he did so in order to oppose the local basing of the US armed forces. Subsequent developments appeared to be playing straight into his hands.

Much contemporary commentary belittled the Shah's designs for the future of his nation, and suggested that the strongman in Tehran was, essentially 'collecting toys of war'. In reality, all the acquisitions in question were based on a series of very careful studies of long-term patterns in modern warfare, and of the requirements for the defence of the Empire; studies conducted by the senior leadership of the Imperial Iranian Armed Forces, educated at the best military educational facilities in the West. Much more than anything else, the 'Shah Factor' was actually based upon the impression made by the Iranian ruler upon Western politicians and the media. They considered Mohammed Reza Shah Pahlavi to be a 'charismatic' and 'impressive' figure striving to rapidly modernise his country, and possessing first-hand knowledge in military affairs – and thus vastly superior to them during any kind of negotiations related to arms purchases. Racism was still prevalent even at the diplomatic level during the 1960s, and in the West it was 'unheard of' for a 'Third World country' to demand sales of advanced weaponry. Under such conditions, the top ranks of the Iranian armed forces became experts in exploiting the negotiating skills and business connections of their ruler to obtain the types of armament thought hopelessly outside their reach only a few years before – and definitely outside the reach of any other countries in the Middle East before, and well after. To their aid came the fact that during the October 1973 Arab-Israeli War, the Organization of the Petroleum Exporting Countries (OPEC) – of which Iran was one of five founding members (together with Iraq, Kuwait, Saudi Arabia, and Venezuela) – significantly reduced its production and imposed an oil blockade upon the Western powers, causing a dramatic increase in oil prices. This was the primary factor enabling countries like Iran and Iraq to massively expand their armed forces during the following years.

EXPANSION OF THE IMPERIAL IRANIAN AIR FORCE

Although a member of CENTO, and despite repeated requests from Tehran, for most of the 1950s and well into the early 1960s, Iran received relatively little military aid from the West. Initially, in addition to some artillery and light tanks for the army, this included a few obsolete minor warships and around 44 Republic P-47D Thunderbolts. By 1961, when the US President John F Kennedy characterised 'the Shah's demands' as 'excessive', Tehran received about two dozen Lockheed T-33A and RT-33A Shooting Star jet trainers and reconnaissance aircraft, 75 Republic F-84G Thunderjet and 24 North American F-86F Sabre jet fighters. However, as the income from oil exports began to increase, Mohammed Reza Shah Pahlavi established links to Tom Jones, Director of the Northrop Corporation, and his representative for the Middle East, Kermit Roosevelt (who was also a close friend of the Shah's brother-in-law and the future commander of the Imperial Iranian Air Force, General Mohammed Khatami). Such connections of a private nature proved instrumental in Iran becoming one of the launching customers for, and then the biggest user worldwide of, Northrop's brand-new F-5A/B Freedom Fighter. Between 1964 and 1970, the Imperial Iranian Air Force (IIAF) was re-equipped with no fewer than 140 of these lightweight, supersonic fighter-bombers.

That was only the beginning, because the senior leadership of the IIAF and the Shah considered the F-5A/B much too short-ranged and poorly armed in comparison to the latest aircraft acquisitions of Iraq. Iran attempted to argue in 1965 that due to their long border with the USSR, and that the latest experience from the Middle East conflicts indicted air power being the dominant discipline, they had a requirement for a squadron-worth of the General Dynamics F-111A. Unimpressed, Washington turned this request down as too complex and costly for the IIAF. Determined to expand their air force with the latest equipment that US industry had to offer, the Iranians then began pushing for delivery of McDonnell-Douglas F-4 Phantom II fighter-bombers, this time declaring their concerns about the safety of the Persian Gulf and its strategic resources. When Washington showed little enthusiasm, the leader in Tehran feinted interest in French-made Dassault Mirage fighter jets. The plot worked: in 1968, Iran and the USA signed a contract for 32 F-4D Phantoms, deliveries of which began about a year later.

For a while afterwards, both the Pentagon and the US Congress attempted to stop such practices and additional sales of high-technology armament to Iran. It was too late: the Shah had learned his lesson, and in the light of the disengagement of US armed forces from the war in Southeast Asia, the US arms industry urgently needed additional orders. In 1969, Iran placed a big order for ZSU-23-4 Shilka self-propelled anti-aircraft guns and 9K32M Strela-2M (ASCC/NATO codename 'SA-7B Grail') man-portable air defence systems (MANPADs) from Moscow. The Americans reacted exactly as expected and the same year, Iran was granted permission to place an order for 32 improved F-4E Phantom IIs. Subsequently, the pace of further acquisitions for the IIAF increased in magnitude. In the light of the British decision to withdraw from all bases and possessions 'east of Suez'; the US decision not to replace the British presence in the Middle East; and the OPEC agreement with 22 major Western oil corporations for greater control over oil production and setting prices from early 1971, Iran's oil revenues doubled in just one year. In July 1971 Tehran secured the agreement of the White House, the Pentagon, and the Congress to place an order for 73 additional F-4Es, for deliveries in 1974–76.

Playing straight into the hands of the Iranians, in April 1972 Baghdad and Moscow then signed the Iraqi-Soviet Friendship Treaty. Originally emphasising cooperation in the field of oil exploration and exploitation, this included the option of Iraq providing basing rights to the Soviet armed forces. Although Baghdad never went as far as to invite or permit stationing of even a single foreign soldier on its soil, this prompted US President Richard B Nixon to make a stop in Tehran and confer with the Shah and his Prime Minister, Amir-Abbas Hoveida, on 30 May 1972. Immediately after, Nixon's National Security Advisor Henry Kissinger announced to the US Congress that henceforth, all purchasing decisions would be left to the Iranian government: henceforth, Tehran was to be granted permission to acquire any conventional weapons it wanted. Iran's reaction was immediate with (amongst other things) the IIAF putting in motion a major expansion project, aiming to establish an integrated air defence system covering the entire country, a network of 14 major air bases and at least 14 major early warning radar stations, all protected by 37 battalions equipped with Hughes MIM-23B I-HAWK surface-to-air missiles (SAMs). Furthermore, Tehran placed a series of major orders with US aerospace companies. In addition to 140 F-5A/Bs and more than 60 Lockheed C-130E/H Hercules transports acquired since 1965, the IIAF was bolstered through procurement of:

- 14 Boeing 707-3J9C and a similar number of Boeing 747s, which served as tankers and transports;
- 169 Northrop F-5E/F Tiger II lightweight fighter-bombers (contract for which was signed in 1972);
- another batch of 36 F-4E Phantom IIs (February 1973);
- the first order for 30 Grumman F-14A Tomcat interceptors (November 1973), and the second for 50 additional Tomcats, together with 784 associated AIM-54A Phoenix long-range air-to-air missiles.

This rush to acquire hardware was accompanied by a rush to train the necessary personnel: while closing its own training facilities – which were too small for the task at hand – the IIAF conducted multiple, large-scale recruiting campaigns and sent dozens of thousands of its cadets for training as flight- and ground crews in the USA. As a result, the air force grew from 7,000 officers and other ranks operating about 75 aircraft in 1965, to almost 100,000 operating nearly 500 aircraft in 1978.

Such explosive growth was possible because Iran's oil revenues continued to increase in magnitude: from US$800 million in 1971 to $1.6 billion in 1972, to $4.6 billion in 1974, and 17.8 billion in 1975. Therefore, in 1974 Tehran – reflecting the concern that it might be subjected to a similar arms embargo like that against Turkey after its invasion of Cyprus – not only placed massive orders for all sorts of spare parts and ammunition (including several thousands of guided air-to-air and air-to-ground missiles) but contracted dozens of Western companies for the construction of elaborate maintenance facilities and factories for all branches of its armed forces, and for all recently ordered weapons systems. These were to enable the Iranian armed forces not only to maintain the US-made aircraft and helicopters of the IIAF, the Imperial Iranian Army and the Imperial Iranian Army Aviation, but also to manufacture spare parts for them, before – in the early 1980s – commencing licence production of selected helicopter types. In similar fashion, the emerging Iranian arms industry was planned to carry out production of all weaponry for aircraft and helicopters, starting with free-fall/general-purpose bombs, but also to include Hughes AGM-65 Maverick electro-optically guided air-to-ground missiles, and AIM-9 Sidewinder infra-red homing air-to-air missiles. Obviously, in a society that was in as woeful state as the Empire of Iran in the early 1970s, where up to 40 percent of the population was still illiterate, and there was an acute shortage of engineers and electronic technicians, for example, this required massive educational programs and the construction of other infrastructure, including roads, railways, the energy supply system, educational and health facilities, apartments, and a further expansion of the oil and gas industry. As a consequence, the Shah's huge military acquisitions in the 1972–78 period prompted a simultaneous and massive reform of society, and a rapid economic development of the entire nation.

IMPERIAL IRANIAN NAVY

In one form or another, the Iranian navy has existed at least since Achaemenid times, about 500 BC, through the era of the Sasanian Empire, the Afsharid and Qajar dynasties, to the Pahlavi times of the 1920s. It was almost completely destroyed during the Anglo-Soviet invasion of 1941, and subsequently rebuilt into a coastal and coast guard service. As of 1947, the Imperial Iranian Navy (IIN) operated only three 16-year-old Italian-built patrol craft in the Persian Gulf, and three in the Caspian Sea. In July 1949, the British-designed landing craft depot ship HMS *Derby Haven* was acquired as the Imperial Iranian Navy Ship (IINS) *Babr* and acted as a 'frigate', as was the Algerine-class minesweeper HMS *Fly*, which became Imperial IINS *Palang*. Both vessels were in poor condition though and paid off by 1966–69.[1]

The IIN experienced only a modest expansion and upgrades during the 1950s and through most of the 1960s. Nine Azar-class coastal patrol boats were acquired between 1954 and 1955, although all had been stricken by the late 1970s. Meanwhile, between 1956 and 1959, they were augmented by four Cape-class patrol craft: the *Keyvan*, *Tiran*, *Mehran* and *Mahan* each had a 40mm Bofors automatic gun, a Mousetrap ASW rocket launcher and could release depth charges, but were equipped with no sonar; nevertheless they were useful vessels which would serve for decades longer.

Between 1959 and 1962, two large infantry landing ships and four MSC 268-class wooden coastal minesweepers – hull numbers 275, 276, 291 and 292 – were transferred to Iran. While the infantry landing ships saw only a short service in Iran, the MSC 268-class were named *Shahbaz*, *Shahrokh*, *Simorgh* and *Karkas* respectively, and all except for *Shahbaz* (lost to a fire in 1975) remained operational into the 1980s.

In 1964, the force of mine-countermeasures (MCM) vessels was strengthened through the acquisition of two Cove-class inshore minesweepers, MSI 13 and MSI 14, named *Kahnamuie* and *Riazi* in Iranian service, respectively (in August 1967, the former was renamed *Harishi*). Finally, between 1967 and 1970, Washington delivered three improved PGM-71-class patrol craft named as *Parwin*, *Bahram*, and *Nahid*, armed with 40mm guns and equipped

IINS *Milanian*, the last of four PF-103-class corvettes constructed for Iran in the USA, seen later in her career, wearing the hull number 83 (originally, this was F27). (Leon Manoucherians collection)

IINS *Harishi*, one of two Cove-class inshore minesweepers, seen sometime between 1976 and 1979. (Photo by Robert Hurst)

IINS *Nahid*, third ship of the class of three PGM-71-class patrol craft with ASW capability. (Leon Manoucherians collection)

with navigational radar, and AN/SQS-17B sonar for rudimentary anti-submarine warfare (ASW) capability.

The first true breakthrough for the IIN came in 1963, when Tehran was granted permission to acquire larger warships in the form of four corvettes of the PF-103-class. Rated as frigates by the IIN,

Bayandor and *Naghdi* were launched in 1963 and completed a year later, while *Milanian* and *Kahnamuie* followed in May and July 1964, and were commissioned to service in February 1969. These diesel-powered general-purpose vessels were armed with two 76mm guns and had a sensor suite including AN/SPS-6 search- and AN/SPG-34 fire-control radars. They had a good ASW capability, centred on their AN/SQS-17 hull-mounted sonar, and Hedgehog mortars for depth charges. In 1965, the IIN acquired the 3,300-ton Battle-class destroyer HMS *Sluys* (D60). The ship was then subjected to a major rebuild by Vosper Thornycroft of Southampton, which included the installation of an AWS-1 search radar, MS-26 sonar, Sea Hunter fire-control radars, and an AN/RDL-1 electronic support measures system. The original armament of four 114mm (4.5in) guns was enhanced through the installation of a launcher for British-made Seacat SAMs. Named *Artemiz* (hull number D5) in IIN service, it took part in the Iranian operation to secure the Tunb Islands on 30 November 1971. However, the IIN was still not entirely satisfied and in 1975 the ship was sent to Cape Town in South Africa, for a refit and another upgrade through the installation of Mk.32 launchers for US-made RIM-66 Standard SM-1MR SAMs.[2]

FRIGATES AND DESTROYERS

The acquisition of *Artemiz* marked the beginning of the first phase of the Iranian naval build-up, which included conversion of the IIN from a 'brown water' – or coastal naval power – into a 'blue water', or ocean-going force, capable of projecting power into the Indian Ocean. Indeed, this destroyer was not yet in Iran when, in August 1966, Tehran placed an order with Vosper Thornycroft for four frigates of the Mk. 5 design. Initially rated as 'destroyer escorts' by the Iranians (and correspondingly assigned hull numbers with the prefix 'DE'), the 'Vospers' were extremely advanced vessels with powerful weapons systems and a high degree of automation, which resulted in a crew of only 125 (compared with a minimum of 133 for each of the four PF-103s). At £6.5 million each, they were cheap (about 66 percent the price of comparable vessels), while powered by an advanced combined diesel or gas (CODOG) propulsion, centred on Rolls-Royce Olympus gas turbines, capable of accelerating them up to 40 knots. Highly reliable Paxman Ventura diesels, renowned for requiring minimal maintenance, were used for cruising. Like *Artemiz*, each of the four Vospers had the Plessey AWS-1 search radar with an identification friend or foe (IFF) system installed, and the Sea Hunter fire-control system, but their hulls housed the Type 170 attack sonar and Type 174 search sonar. The weapons suite included a quintuple launcher for Italian-made Seakiller Mk.2 anti-ship missiles, and a triple launcher for British-made Sea Cat SAMs,

A front view of IINS *Artemiz*, seen after her upgrade through the installation of launchers for RIM-66 Standard SM-1MR SAMs (visible adjacent to the bridge). (Leon Manoucherians collection)

A side-view of IINS *Artemiz* in the late 1970s, with all modifications added according to Iranian orders. (Leon Manoucherians collection)

a triple-barrelled Mark 10 Limbo Anti-Submarine Mortar, a Mark 8 Mod 0 114mm gun, and one twin 35mm Oerlikon Bührle. Named *Saam* (DE12), *Zaal* (DE14), *Rostam* (DE16), and *Faramarz* (DE18), the four frigates were completed between May 1971 and May 1972, and then refitted in Great Britain again between 1975 and 1977, when each received the latest version of the 114mm gun and underwent other work.[3]

The new frigates were not in Iran by the time the IIN placed an order for two even bigger vessels: in March 1971 and February 1972, it received two destroyers of the Allen M. Sumner-class from the USA. Originally, these were USS *Gainard* (DD-706) and USS *Stormes* (DD-780), but when the Iranians found out that *Gainard* was suffering serious mechanical problems, the Americans replaced it with USS *Zellars* (DD-777). Both *Zellars* and *Stormes* were constructed during the Second World War but while still in service with the USN were significantly rebuilt and modernised under the Fleet Rehabilitation and Modernisation II (FRAM II) project. This saw their AN/SQS-4 sonar being augmented with a variable-depth sonar, the installation of two triple Mk.32 launchers for Mk.46 lightweight anti-submarine torpedoes, and removal of all obsolete anti-aircraft artillery. Before joining the IIN as IINS *Babr* (ex-*Zellars*) and IINS *Palang* (ex-*Stormes*), they underwent another overhaul and received improved air conditioning, modern electrical generators, and improved accommodation for a crew of 290.

Before their delivery to Iran, their second Mk.38 turret with twin 127 guns and heavy launchers for anti-ship torpedoes were removed: the former were replaced by four Mk.32 launchers for RIM-66 Standard SM-1MRs, and the latter were replaced by a telescopic hangar designed in Canada, and a helicopter deck wide enough to accommodate medium-sized helicopters. Moreover, each ship received ASW armament in the form of two triple launchers for

The launcher of the GSW.21 Seacat SAM system, as installed on IINS *Artemiz*. The Seacat missile, of which four are visible, weighed 68kg on launch, carried an 18kg warhead, had a maximum range of 5,000m, and was radar-cued but manually controlled. (Leon Manoucherians collection)

The IINS *Saam*, the first in the class of four Vosper Mk. 5-class frigates designed and constructed for the IIN in 1966–72. Notable is her original hull designation, DE12: subsequently, all four ships were re-classified as frigates. (Leon Manoucherians collection)

An elevated view of IINS *Palang* as of the late 1970s. Clearly visible are all four Mk.32 Mod 2 launchers (two near the bridge and two mid-ship), the telescopic hangar, and two turrets with twin 127mm guns. (Leon Manoucherians collection)

RIM-66A STANDARD SM-1

The RIM-66 Standard SM-1MR surface-to-air missile was developed for the USN from 1963. Gradually, it evolved into a family of missiles replacing almost everything that had been used by this service at earlier times, including RIM-2 Terrier, RIM-8 Talos, and RIM-24 Tartar SAMs. Based on the RIM-24C, and closely resembling it, the Standard was a solid-fuel-powered, medium-range weapon (which is why it also became known as 'Standard MR') with monopulse semi-active radar homing, as yet without command or inertial mid-course guidance introduced on subsequent variants.

Weighing 707kg (1,558lbs) on launch, the SM-1MR was 4.72m (15ft 6in) long, it carried the Mk.51 blast fragmentation warhead weighing 52kg, and was equipped with a radar and contact fuse. Its most advanced sub-variant as of the 1970s was the Block IV, which entered series production in 1968, and had a shorter minimum engagement envelope and improved electronic counter-countermeasures (ECCM).

Iran acquired standards in two batches: in 1974, it received 16 RIM-66B, followed by 128 RIM-66Bs in 19768–78. As operated by the IIN, the weapon was guided to the target by the same Mk.25 fire-control system that was also used for gun control. Due to the lack of space, *Artemiz*, *Babr*, and *Palang* each only carried one Mk.25: this could only guide one SM-1MR at a time as the seeker head of the RIM-66B version required continuous target illumination. Considering a supersonic aircraft could reach the ship within 80 seconds of detection, this meant that only one, perhaps two SM-1MRs could be launched in time to stop it. Moreover, while they could be elevated prior to firing, the four Mk.32 Mod 2 launchers were all fixed in their position, meaning that the ship had to turn into the threat for effective deployment of the missiles.

The destroyer IINS *Palang* (D62) seen test-firing a single RIM-66A Standard SM-1MR. (Tom Cooper collection)

A RIM-66 Standard SM-1MR climbing out of one of the forward launchers of IINS *Badr* (D7), releasing its characteristic plume of white smoke. (Leon Manoucherians collection)

Mk.46 lightweight torpedoes, in addition to retaining its Hedgehog mortar. *Babr* and *Palang* also retained their SPS-20 early warning radar with a maximum range of around 240nm (445km) – and a practical detection range for fighter-jet-sized aircraft of about 100nm (185km) – and the SPS-10 surface search radar. The SQS-4 sonar was replaced by AN/SQS-43 on *Babr*, and SQS-44 on *Palang*, and both were equipped with an AN/SQQ-10 variable-depth sonar. Finally, both vessels retained their FRAM II electronic warfare suite, including an AN/WLR-1 electronic support measures (ESM) system and AN/ULQ-6 electronic countermeasures (ECM) system, as well as an AN/UPX-12 IFF system. As such, these destroyers were more powerful than many contemporary vessels of the US Navy. They were commissioned into the IIN on 14 October 1973, and departed for Iran a few days later, sailing around Africa because the Suez Canal was still closed.

BUILD-UP OF TFB.6 IN BUSHEHR

Tehran understood that the Allen M Sumner-class destroyers would need embarked helicopters, and that modern sea power was ineffective without air support. Aiming to obtain the capability to support its warships not only inside the Persian Gulf but in the north-western Indian Ocean, during the first half of the 1970s Tehran invested heavily in bolstering its military presence along the coast. A major air base was constructed outside the port of Bushehr in the early 1970s, subsequently expanded through the construction of two early warning radar stations, two MIM-23B I-HAWK SAM sites, and was then elevated to the status of Tactical Fighter Base 6 (TFB.6). By 1976, no fewer than three fighter-bomber units were worked up there, each equipped with 16 F-4Es: the 61st, 62nd, and 63rd Tactical Fighter Squadrons (TFS). The pace of their operations was very intensive: each unit averaged 20 sorties a day, with most pilots clocking between 260 and 300 hours of flying time a year. Up to 50 percent of this flying time was dedicated to training in anti-ship operations, primarily with the use of AGM-65A Maverick air-to-surface missiles, 2,850 of which were purchased from the USA. At least four F-4Es – each armed with two AIM-7E-2 Sparrow and four AIM-9J Sidewinder air-to-air missiles – were held on around-the-clock quick reaction alert. TFB.3 also became a hub for operations of up to six McDonnell-Douglas RF-4E Phantom II reconnaissance fighters of the 11th Tactical Reconnaissance Squadron (TRS), homebased at Mehrabad (TFB.1; in Tehran): these flew reconnaissance sorties over the entire Persian Gulf, regularly over Oman, and sometimes ranged deep over Iraq and Saudi Arabia.

IMPERIAL IRANIAN NAVAL AVIATION

Meanwhile, the IIN was working-up its own flying branch – the Imperial Iranian Naval Aviation (IINA). By 1972, this was a small service mainly for liaison and transportation, equipped with six Rockwell Shrike Commander light transports and 14 Italian-

Table 3: Known Iranian Agusta-Bell AB.212ASW Helicopters		
Construction Number	IINA Serial Number	Notes
5508	6-2401	
5510	6-2402	
5513	6-2403	
5515	6-2404	
5517	6-2405	
5518	6-2406	
5536	6-2407	
5539	6-2410	collided with high power wires, Shatt al-Arab, 20 Sep 1980
??	6-2411	
5541	6-2412	
??	6-2413	
5543	6-2414	crashed near Bushehr on 13 August 2014
5544	6-2415	
5545	6-2416	
??	6-2417	
??	6-2420	

Although taken at TFB.7 (Shiraz) in 1977, during the CENTO exercise NIDLINK '77 – conducted in cooperation with the US Air Force and the US Navy – this photograph of an F-4E of the IIAF is representative of the appearance and equipment of TFB.6's F-4Es during the war with Iraq. The jet wears the same camouflage pattern and almost the same insignia as those based in Bushehr, and is armed with a single AGM-65A Maverick electro-optically guided air-to-ground missile (visible underneath the cockpit area). (Tom Cooper collection)

An Agusta-Bell AB.212ASW helicopter of the IINA seen in a high-speed turn, armed with an LAU-3 pod for 68mm unguided rockets. (IRINA Photo)

torpedoes, or two depth charges. Moreover, several Iranian AB.212ASWs had the SMA/APS search radar installed in a large black dome above the cockpit, and all received installations for French-designed AS.12 anti-tank guided missiles (ATGMs), LAU-3A and AERA HL-12-70 pods for unguided rockets, and GPU-2A gun pods with a six-barrel 20mm automatic cannon. The unit flying them was homebased at the newly constructed Naval Air Station (NAS) Bandar Abbas, but later moved to NAS Bushehr, and had single helicopters periodically deployed aboard *Babr* and *Palang*.

manufactured Agusta-Bell AB.206A helicopters. In the same year, the service received its first major reinforcements through an order for 20 of the then brand-new Agusta-Bell AB.212ASW helicopters. This was a more powerful (twin-engined) version of the well-known Bell 212 (developed from the ubiquitous Bell 205/UH-1 Huey family), but custom-tailored for anti-submarine warfare. Most examples delivered to Iran had the SMA/APS surface search radar and installations for armament such as two Mk.46 lightweight

IRANIAN ORIONS

In September 1971, the Iranian Ministry of Defence made the decision to acquire Lockheed P-3 Orion maritime patrol aircraft with an operational range of 1,245nm (2,306km). Following extensive negotiations, in January 1972 Tehran and Washington signed a contract for six aircraft, a multi-year spares package, ground-support

The last of six Lockheed P-3F Orions destined for Iran (original IIAF serial 5-261), in its original livery, with the upper half of the fuselage in white, lower half and wings in gull gray, with IIAF-titles and pre-1976 serials, seen before delivery. (Milpix/Martin Hornliman collection)

Photographed on the same occasion at NAS Moffet Field, this was the first of six P-3Fs destined for Iran (IIAF serial number 5-256) – and the first to receive the unique camouflage pattern, applied on Iranian request and only on their Orions. (Milpix/Martin Hornliman collection)

In 1978, the second Iranian P-3F was sent to the USA for test installation of the AGM-84A Harpoon missile. By that time it had a new serial – 5-8702 – and is shown in this photograph with a Harpoon on the inboard underwing pylon. (Tom Cooper collection)

equipment and training worth US$97.7 million. Additional contracts were drawn up for the construction of a suitable base near the port of Bandar-e Abbas. The construction of the resulting Tactical Fighter Base 9 (TFB.9) advanced relatively quickly and transports of the US Air Force made extensive use of this facility during the October 1973 Arab-Israeli War, when they stopped to refuel there while underway to Israel with loads of ammunition and spares from Iranian stocks. Simultaneously, and under the guise of 'familiarising Iranian air force crews with the type', the US Navy deployed two of its own P-3Cs at TFB.9, which were used to patrol the Hormuz Straits. Concluding that not only the P-3s, but also the Strait needed suitable protection, the IIAF then went a step further and placed an order for two squadrons-worth of additional F-4E Phantom IIs.

A close-up photograph of the second Iranian P-3F, showing the installation of the underwing pylon and an ATM-84A Harpoon training round. (Tom Cooper collection)

For the purpose of delivering Orions to Iran, the US Navy took six P-3Bs from its surplus stocks and outfitted them to a unique standard: their AN/APS-115 surface search radars and basic mission system with side-by-side working stations, undernose surveillance cameras, and externally-loaded sonobuoy tubes were all retained. However, they received the ARN-84 TACAN navigational system and APN-153 Doppler from the P-3C variant and had the navigator's station moved to the port side. The result was the variant designated P-3F and exported to Iran only. Crews of the IIAF began training with USN patrol squadron VP-31 at NAS Moffet Field in February 1975, and the first deliveries of P-3Fs to Iran took place in April 1975. Three months later, the unit slated to operate them – the 91st Anti-Submarine Warfare Squadron (ASWS), IIAF – was officially established and declared operational at TFB.9.

In 1976, the TFB.9 was reinforced through the arrival of 36 additional F-4Es – the last Phantoms acquired by Iran. The first 18 of these entered service with the newly established 91st TFS, nicknamed 'the Sharks'. Although Iran eventually collected all the jets from this order, the second unit slated to become operational at TFB.9 – the 92nd TFS – was never officially established: instead, its 18 mounts were stored. Supported by about 80 US advisors, the 91st ASWS and the 91st TFS were worked up in the course of a series of tactical exercises that emphasised anti-ship warfare: this effort peaked in February 1977, when they took part in a joint exercise with F-14As from TFB.8, and a carrier battle group of the US Navy, centred on the nuclear-powered aircraft carrier USS Enterprise

Table 4: Lockheed P-3F Orion Maritime Patrol Aircraft of Iran[4]			
Bureau Number	Original IIAF Serial Number	IIAF/IRIAF Serial Number since 1 January 1976	Notes
159342	5-256	5-8701	
159343	5-257	5-8702	adapted for AGM-84A in 1978, crashed at Shiraz on 15 February 1984
159344	5-258	5-8702	
159345	5-259	5-8703	
159346	5-260	5-8704	
159347	5-261	5-8705	

(CVN-65), escorted by nuclear-powered guided missile cruisers USS *Long Beach* (CGN-9) and USS *Truxtun* (CGN-35).

Highly satisfied with TFB.9 and its units rapidly reaching their initial operational capability, in 1978, Tehran placed an order for three additional P-3Fs, expressed its intention to acquire nine more, and ordered its entire Orion-fleet to be equipped with AGM-84 Harpoon anti-ship missiles. For this purpose, one airframe was flown to the USA to serve as a test-ship for the required installations. The aircraft and several Harpoons were returned to Iran by the end of the same year, but additional P-3s and the full order of AGM-84s were never delivered. Even if never operating F-4s nor P-3s, the IIN thus had a strong combat component on its side, deployed where it mattered the most.

FOKKERS, SEA STALLIONS AND SEA KINGS

Meanwhile, in 1975–76, the IIN acquired four Fokker F.27 transports (including two F.27-400Ms and two F.27-600s) and placed an order for six of the big Sikorsky RH-53D Sea Stallion helicopters. While the Fokkers belonged to relatively simple variants that served for transport and liaison, the RH-53Ds retained all the basic systems of the earlier CH-53s, but also had removable minesweeping gear: alternatively, they could carry 37 passengers or 15,622lbs (7,086kg) of cargo.

Finally, aiming to equip and work-up a unit that could provide helicopters for bigger warships, the acquisition of which was already in process (see below for details), in 1976 the IIN placed an order for 20 Agusta-Sikorsky ASH-3D helicopters: essentially a version of the Sikorsky SH-3D Sea King of the US Navy, manufactured under licence in Italy, but having a reinforced cell and more powerful engines, also known under the designation AS.61. They were delivered in two batches starting in 1978 and could be armed with up to four Mk.44 or Mk.46 lightweight torpedoes, or four depth charges. In the same year, Tehran requested their modification to carry Italian-made Oto Melara Marte anti-ship guided missiles – an air-launched version of the Sea Killer that was meanwhile in the process of being installed on all four Vosper-made frigates – with a range of 25km. To improve their ability to detect and track targets for Martes, the second batch of ASH-3Ds built for Iran was equipped with a bigger surface search radar installed in a housing under the fuselage. However, the work on re-equipping Iranian Sea Kings was interrupted by the revolution of 1978–79, and never completed during the war with Iraq.

EARLY OPERATIONS

Encouraged by the latest acquisitions, the IIN then switched its attention to the second phase of its expansion project, aiming to make it the dominant navy not only in the Persian Gulf but in the Indian Ocean too: indeed, one that was to outmatch even the Indian Navy. Correspondingly, in November 1972, the Shah of Iran announced his intention of expanding the IIN 'five times' and 'extending Iran's security perimeter to the north-western Indian Ocean'.[5] Considering his navy was short on experienced crews – and especially on the technical ratings necessary for all its new and large

An IINA Fokker F.27 seen at Abadan Airport in 1977, by when all had this grey overall camouflage pattern. (Consultair, via Tom Cooper)

A pre-delivery photograph of the third RH-53D Sea Stallion mine-clearing helicopter acquired by the IINA in 1975–76. The full Iranian serial number was 9-2703. (Tom Cooper collection)

vessels – this, at the time, 'unusual' announcement surprised many in the West. However, both the Vospers and the three destroyers proved popular in service and were soon active both in the Persian Gulf and Indian Ocean. Any possible deficiencies were rapidly ironed out by intensive training (frequently in cooperation with the Royal and US navies), and numerous cruises, some of which brought Iranian warships all the way to Singapore. Indeed, they saw their first action in 1974, when involved in supporting the counterinsurgency campaign in Oman, where all three destroyers and the Vospers repeatedly conducted naval gunfire support operations against shore targets, in cooperation with the Iranian Marines and naval helicopters deployed there.[6] In turn, this experience taught the IIN about the necessity to acquire underway replenishment ships, necessary to support warships operating away from homeports. Correspondingly, in 1974, two replenishment vessels were acquired from West Germany, and commissioned into service as *Bandar Abbas* and *Bushehr*.

Given the heavy ASW armament of all seven new Iranian warships, and the absence of submarines in other navies of the Middle East, there were many wondering about their actual purpose. However, the Shah made it clear, publicly, and several times, that he had grandiose ambitions for this country, which he considered an emerging great power capable of imposing Pax Iranica on the Persian Gulf – and that his pretensions were not limited to this area alone. When in 1974 the Indian Prime Minister Indira Gandhi called for a zone of peace in the Indian Ocean, the Iranian leader announced his own plan for the region, including developing the Empire of Iran into a major military power and industrial giant, capable of influencing affairs all over the Middle East and Southeast Asia. The Algiers Accord symbolised Iran's supremacy in the Gulf, and neighbouring Arab countries had no means to counter it: more distant powers apparently followed in fashion. Although the Shah's operational goals were less clear, the Westerners and their Arab allies on the western side of the Persian Gulf, had second thoughts about this development. For example, London warned that the Iranian ruler was suffering delusions of grandeur, while the Defense Intelligence Agency of the USA suggested that he might embark upon military adventures of his own design once Iran had completed its military build-up, in around 1980. However, the Shah countered that he needed a strong navy in order to counter the presence of Soviet Navy in the area, and all the critics fell silent.

SERIAL NUMBERS OF IRANIAN COMBAT AIRCRAFT

Traditionally, Iranian military aircraft are prominent for their serial numbers. In the 1920s and 1930s, these were applied in the form of two- and then three-digit numbers, usually on the ruder of the aircraft. When the IIAF was rebuilt following the Second World War, a practice was introduced of applying serial numbers consisting of a single-digit prefix, apparently denoting the purpose of the aircraft, followed by a two-digit suffix, denoting individual airframes (for example: 2-85 for one of their P-47s). As the air force continued to grow, in the 1960s this system was expanded to a single-digit prefix, followed by a three-digit suffix. Finally, effective from 1 January 1976, the current system was introduced, with a single-digit prefix, followed by a four-digit suffix, where the prefix denoted the purpose of the aircraft (for example: 2 for training and reconnaissance; 3 for combat; 5 for transport; 6, 8 and 9 for helicopters; and 7 for training aircraft), and the suffix denoted individual aircraft. Generally, this system has been retained up to the present time, but bigger fleets of certain types have been re-serialled several times since – whether to cover up losses or to confuse foreign observers. Moreover, there were several exceptions from the rules regarding prefixes: for example, the prefix 2 was originally reserved for training aircraft, but applied on RF-5As and then RF-4Es of the early 1970s because these were involved in joint, clandestine US-Iranian reconnaissance operations deep inside Soviet airspace. The reason why the Iranian P-3F fleet was prefixed with 5- (a sequence used by transports like Boeing CH-47C Chinook helicopters, Boeing 707 and 747 tankers, and Lockheed C-130 Hercules) remains unclear.

A zoomed-in section of a photograph showing details of the serial number on the fin of a P-3F, as applied from 1 January 1976. Visible above the fin flash is the service title. On IINA/IRINA aircraft and helicopters, this meant Imperial Iranian Navy before 1979 and means Islamic Republic of Iran Navy after 1979; on IIAF/IRIAF aircraft and helicopters it meant Imperial Iranian Air Force before 1979, and Islamic Republic of Iran Air Force ever since. (US Navy Photo)

LA COMBATTANTE II

Before embarking upon more ambitious projects, in February 1973 the IIN placed an order for six La Combattante II-class fast attack craft (FAC) with the Constructions Mécaniques de Normandie (CMN) shipyard in

The IINS *Kaman*, the lead ship of the Kaman-class as the La Combattante II-class was named in Iran. Clearly visible are the turret with 76mm gun forward, the large dome for the antenna of the Signaal WM 28 weapons system and four canisters for Harpoon missiles. (Leon Manoucherians collection)

Mohammad Reza Shah Pahlavi, wearing the uniform of an Admiral of the Imperial Iranian Navy, seen inspecting Iranian Marines. (Amir Kiani collection)

Cherbourg. A follow-up order from October 1974 added another six vessels of this type. What the Iranians named the Kaman-class, were 275-ton diesel-powered but very fast ships, equipped with the Signaal WM 28 weapons system, including Thomson-CSF Alligator 5A ECM and DR2000 Dalia ESM systems, and armed with one Oto Melara automatic 76mm gun and four launchers for BGM-84 Harpoon anti-ship missiles. The first nine vessels – *Kaman, Zoubin, Khadang, Peykan, Joshan, Falakhon, Shamshir, Gorz,* and *Gardouneh* – were all commissioned to service between August 1977 and September 1978. However, because of the Iranian failure to pay for them, the last three – *Kanjar, Neyzeh,* and *Tabrazin* – were held back in Cherbourg until 15 August 1981. For their equipment, Iran placed an order for 60 Harpoon missiles in the USA, but only nine of these were delivered before February 1979.

The Kaman-class proved to be versatile vessels, packing almost the same punch as bigger frigates and destroyers: it was only their shorter range and lesser ammunition capacity that made them weaker. Moreover, their acquisition was accompanied by an order worth US$54 million from October 1974, placed with Swan Hunter of Great Britain, for a modified Ol-class replenishment ship. The result was the 33,014 ton (full load) tanker named *Khark*, armed with a single 76mm Oto Melara and two 40mm guns (which were never fitted), but also having a helipad that could accept helicopters the size of the RH-53D, and two large hangars for three helicopters the size of ASH-3Ds. *Khark* was launched in February 1977, and began trials in November 1978, but then experienced problems and delays: in August 1979, the order was almost cancelled, but the Iranians then pressed on and commissioned the ship into service. Nevertheless, London refused to issue an export licence because of the outbreak of the war with Iraq, and thus *Khark* reached Bandar Abbas only in October 1984. Unknown to all those involved, this was to become the last major surface vessel of Western origin to reinforce Iran's fleet.[7]

SPARES AND KNOW-HOW

Like the Imperial Iranian Air Force, so also the IIN planned to obtain both the capability to maintain and support its fleet on its own in the event of a Western arms embargo. Correspondingly, in addition to acquiring the latest technology from the USA and its allies, in 1974 it embarked on purchasing two Gearing-class destroyers of the

USS *Amphion* (AR-13) while still in service with the USN. The ship was renamed IINS *Chabahar* once it was commissioned into service with the Imperial Iranian Navy, and proved of crucial importance for the Iranian capability to maintain its warships during the war with Iraq. (Leon Manoucherians collection)

of coastal surveillance and air defence radars was operational by early 1979.

UNREALISED PROJECTS

The massive build-up of the Imperial Iranian Navy during the early-1970s was still 'just the beginning': only the first phase of the navy's expansion programme. During the middle of the same decade, the IIN entered the second phase, during which it planned to further bolster its fleet through the acquisition of attack submarines, modern destroyers, and frigates. Eventually, Tehran's resulting shopping spree of 1974–78 surpassed even the projected growth of the Imperial Iranian Air Force.

In 1974, Tehran placed an order for six guided missile destroyers in the USA. Based on the hulls of the Spruance-class – which was in the process of entering service with the USN at the time – they retained its two 127mm guns and ASW capabilities – including the AN/SQS-33 sonar and a pair of triple launchers for Mk.46 torpedoes – but added significantly bolstered air defence capacity. The centrepieces of the latter were the AN/SPQ-9 and AN/SPG-51 weapons systems, supported by the powerful AN/SPS-48 3D-radar, serving two twin-rail Mk.26 launchers for much improved RIM-66C Standard SM-2 SAMs and RUR-5 Anti-Submarine Rockets (ASROC). Moreover, they had heavy-duty air conditioning plants, dust separators on their gas turbine intakes, and an increased water distillation capacity, all for more effective operations in the Middle East. The resulting Kouroush-class (including *Kourosh*/D11, *Dariush*/D12, *Nader*/D13, *Anoshirvan*/D14, *Shapour*/D15 and *Ardeshir*/D16) was still under construction when, in June 1976, the order was downsized to four (i.e. *Shapour* and *Ardeshir* were cancelled) because of their rapidly increasing costs (from US$120 to 338 million per vessel) caused by high inflation in the USA. Before any could be delivered, the Shah was toppled and this contract cancelled: instead, the resulting four powerful destroyers were completed and taken into service by the USN as the Kidd-class.

A similar fate befell the Iranian attempt to acquire nuclear-powered attack submarines of the Sturgeon-class (SSN-637).[8] Instead, the Shah was offered – and accepted – three diesel-electric submarines of the Tang-class: USS *Tang* (SS-563), USS *Wahoo* (SS-565), and USS *Trout* (SS-566). Following extensive overhaul and training, the first of them, *Trout*, was handed over to an IIN crew as *Kousseh*, at New London on 19 December 1978, but the contract was cancelled in February–March 1979, before any could reach Iran. The same was true for six Type 209-class submarines under construction at the Howaldtswerke-Deutsche Werft in Germany since March 1978, and 12 NATO Standard Frigates (based on the design of the Koertaner-class constructed in the Netherlands) – of which four were to be constructed by the Bremer Vulkan shipyard,

USN: USS *Kenneth D Bailey* (DD-713) and sister ship USS *Bordelon* (DD-881). Both were acquired as scrap, but: they had a high degree of commonality in parts with the Allen M Sumner-class, and thus provided the Iranian navy with the opportunity to learn to use them as sources of spares, and thus continue maintaining its destroyers without US support. As soon as the two arrived in Iran in July 1977, both were moored and then systematically stripped of all useful parts. For similar reasons, Tehran then acquired the repair ship USS *Amphion* (AR-13): this was named *Chabahar* in Iranian service. Next, the USN loaned the 150-metre-long floating dock USS *Arco* to the IIN: this had the Iranian hull number 400, and was to prove one of the most valuable purchases ever made by Tehran for decades to come.

Despite the construction of new major facilities, Khorramshahr on the Shatt al-Arab, near Basra in Iraq, remained the main naval base of the IIN until 1977 – although obviously too exposed. In that year, most major vessels were moved to the newly constructed installation in Bandar-e Abbas, which included two dry docks, the sole floating dry dock, the sole repair ship, and the new Fleet Maintenance Unit designed and managed by the Danish engineering consultant Kompsax of Copenhagen, but largely run by a number of British companies. This base was planned to become capable of providing maintenance facilities (with overhaul capability) for marine gas turbines, hovercraft and other major vessels of the navy, and these were all already under construction. The port in Bushehr also included a small shipyard, used for maintenance purposes only. The main supply centres were developed in Khorramshahr and Bandar-e Shahpur, but the navy had no dedicated oil storage facilities: instead, it depended on NIOC for the supply of fuel and lubricating oils. Finally, the development of the major naval communications network – Project Morvarid, which was to link all the bases and ships – was never completed, although a chain

Table 5: Names and Hull Numbers of IRIN Warships, 1966–1979

Name	Hull Number	Notes
	01	SR.N6
	02	SR.N6
	03	SR.N6
	04	SR.N6
	05	SR.N6
	06	SR.N6
	07	SR.N6
	08	SR.N6
Shahbaz	21	minesweeper
	22	minesweeper
Shahrokh	23	minesweeper
Palang	24	minesweeper
	27	LST
	31	LST
	32	LST
Simorgh	33	LST
	34	LST
Sohrab	44	LST
	46	LST
Artemiz	51 (ex D5)	destroyer; renamed *Damavand*
	52	destroyer
Babr	61 (ex 7)	destroyer
Palang	62 (ex 9)	destroyer
Saam	71 (ex DE12)	frigate; renamed *Alvand*
Zaal	72 (ex DE14)	renamed *Alborz*
Rostam	73 (ex DE16)	renamed *Sabalan*
Faramarz	74 (ex DE18)	renamed *Sahand*
Bayandor	81 (ex F25)	corvette
Naghdi	82 (ex F26)	corvette
Milanian	83 (ex F27)	corvette
Kahnamuie	84 (ex F28)	corvette
	101	BH.7
	102	BH.7
	103	BH.7
	104	BH.7
	105	BH.7
	106	BH.7
Nahid	122	patrol boat
Keyvan	201 (ex 61)	large patrol craft
Tiran	202 (ex 62)	large patrol craft
Mehran	203 (ex 63)	large patrol craft
Mahan	204 (ex 64)	large patrol craft
Parvin	211	large patrol craft
Bahram	212	large patrol craft
Nahid	213	large patrol craft
Kaman	P221	fast patrol craft
Xoubin	P222	fast patrol craft
Khadang	P223	fast patrol craft
Peykan	P224	fast patrol craft
Joshan	P225	fast patrol craft
Falakhon	P226	fast patrol craft
Shamshir	P227	fast patrol craft
Gorz	P228	fast patrol craft
Gardouneh	P229	fast patrol craft
Khanjar	P230	fast patrol craft; delivered in August 1981
Neyzeh	P231	fast patrol craft
Tabarzin	P232	fast patrol craft
	255	PBR Mk III
	265	PBR Mk III
Shahrokh	275	coastal minesweeper
Hamzeh	276	coastal minesweeper
Simorgh	291	coastal minesweeper
Karkas	292	coastal minesweeper
Harishi	301	minesweeper
Lavan	401	light auxiliary ship
Hormuz	402	light auxiliary ship
Kish	403	light auxiliary ship
Kangan	411	auxiliary water tanker
Taheri	412	auxiliary water tanker
Shahid Marnaji		auxiliary water tanker
Amir		auxiliary water tanker
Bandar Abbas	421	replenishment ship
Bushehr	422	replenishment ship
Deylam	424	water carrier
Khark	431	replenishment ship; under construction, delivered in Oct 1984
Delvar	471	ammunition ship
Sirjan	472	ammunition ship
Charak	481	cargo ship
Chiroo	482	cargo ship
Souru	482	cargo ship
Dayer		support ship
Hengam	511	heavy landing ship
Larak	512	heavy landing ship
Tonb	513	under construction, delivered in February 1985

and the others at the Rhine-Schelde-Verolme, in Holland – were all cancelled after the fall of the Shah.

Another, even more advanced phase of the IIN's growth was still a topic of several major studies and negotiations as of late 1978: reportedly, it included the acquisition of a small aircraft carrier of the Sea Control Ship (SCS) design: a 13,736 ton vessel carrying a

USS *Kidd*, shortly after entering service with the USN in 1980. The ship was originally ordered by Iran as IINS *Koroush* (hull number D11). Notable are turrets for automatic 127mm guns, two Mk.26 twin-rail launchers for RIM-66C Standard SM-2 SAMs, and the large helicopter deck with a hangar that was wider than that on usual Spruance-class destroyers. (Leon Manoucherians collection)

An invitation for the decommissioning and transfer ceremony of USS *Trout*, which became IINS *Kousseh* in IIN service. The contract was cancelled only two months later, and thus Iran never received its first submarine. (Leon Manoucherians collection)

combination of ASW helicopters and either British- or US-made short take-off/vertical landing jets – probably a version of the famous Hawker Siddeley/British Aerospace Sea Harrier. Because of the latter, in competition was also a vessel of the British-designed Invincible-class.[9] Obviously, nothing of this was ever realised (even if Spain subsequently did construct a single aircraft carrier based on the SCS design, and commissioned it to service as *Dedalo*, in the mid-1980s). Part of the reason was that Iran's profligate spending came under threat as oil prices began to decline in the late 1970s: rapidly expanding production in the Persian Gulf area was showing its effects. In January 1976, an Iranian delegation led by Vice Minister of Defence, General Hassan Toufanian, complained to the US Secretary of Defence, Donald R. Rumsfeld, that the unit prices of warships ordered by Iran had more than doubled, that the price for Project Peace Shield (MIM-23B I-HAWK) more than tripled, and that the order for communication programmes Seek Switch and Seek Sentry (the latter included seven Boeing E-3A Sentry Airborne Early Warning and Control aircraft) would have to be dramatically curtailed. Nevertheless, Tehran continued placing additional orders through 1977–78 – including one for 160 General Dynamics F-16A/B Fighting Falcon fighter-bombers and another for AGM-45 Shrike anti-radar missiles, and Washington hardly ever complained through 1978.

In the light of shortages of qualified personnel, and the fact that all these arms acquisitions required the presence of up to 100,000 foreign contractors and military advisors, many observers doubt the Iranian capability to ever man all the equipment that was on order as of early 1979, let alone to deploy it effectively without foreign support. The principal reason for this were never-ending complaints about all sorts of Iranian 'incompatibilities' with the Western mindset and high-technologies. However, it should be kept in mind that such doubts were mainly spread by foreign contractors who had a huge commercial interest in extending their contracts. As subsequent developments were to show, Iran actually had enough personnel to man all of its aircraft and warships during the war with Iraq. Indeed, the number of sailors recruited for the IIN reached such levels that even in 1977, the service was short on accommodation for them. A short term solution for this issue was found through the purchase of two disused transatlantic liners from Italy: *Michelangelo* and *Raffaello*. Both ships arrived in Iran under their own power, but were then converted into floating barracks with their own desalinisation plants, and a capacity of 1,800 sailors. *Michelangelo* was moored in Bandar-e Abbas, and *Raffaello* in Bushehr, and a team of about 50 Italian technicians helped maintain them.

HOVERCRAFT FLEET

Searching for a vessel suitable for anti-smuggling operations, the Imperial Iranian Navy became interested in the British-designed hovercraft technology, which was also promising for amphibious warfare. In 1970, Tehran ordered six British Hovercraft Corporation BH.7 vessels of the Wellington-class. The first two, 101 and 102, were delivered by March 1971, and belonged to the Mk. 4 logistic support version with a 14–tonne payload. The remainder – vessels with hull numbers 103, 104, 105, and 106 – were of the BH.7 Mk. 5 version, capable of carrying a 50-tonne payload, and were scheduled to receive the US-made BGM-84 Harpoon anti-ship missiles in the early 1980s. Furthermore, between 1973 and 1975, Iran acquired eight slightly smaller British Hovercraft Corporation SR.N6 Winchester-class vessels (hull numbers 01 to 08), each of which was capable of carrying an 11-tonne payload: they were originally envisaged as missile platforms, but the lack of suitable weapons rendered them to amphibious support. Together, BH.7s and SR.N6s made the IIN one of the biggest military operators of hovercraft: the fleet was consolidated into a squadron commanded by Prince Shahriar Shafiq and homebased in Khosrow Abad, south of Abadan. Several of them saw action in November 1971, clearly demonstrating their capability to rapidly transport troops and equipment. Subsequently, the unit

The first group of Iranian hovercraft pilots, seen in Great Britain in 1970. Visible behind them is one of IIN's SR.N6 hovercraft. (Leon Manoucherians collection)

The second of six Wellington-class BH.7 hovercraft manufactured by the British Hovercraft Corporation for the IINA wore the hull number 102 (unlike ships, Iranian hovercraft were never named). It belonged to the Mk. 4 sub-variant, which was constructed as a logistic support vehicle. It was 24m long and almost 14m wide, had an empty weight of 18.3 tonnes and a displacement of 56 tonnes, and its single Rolls-Royce Marine Proteus 15M gas turbine could accelerate it to the speed of 58 knots (107km/h). (Leon Manoucherians collection)

was regularly deployed for maritime patrols and search and rescue operations.

AMPHIBIOUS WARFARE FLEET

Preoccupied with the acquisition of major surface combatants and aerial support, the IIN was slow in developing its other capabilities, especially a branch capable of amphibious warfare. In 1972 it ordered the construction of four tank landing ships from the Yarrow Yard in Great Britain. All were based on a modified design of the Sir Lancelot-class of the Royal Navy: while displacing 2,540 tons, they could carry 700 tons of cargo, including 9 to 12 main battle tanks and 230 troops, and land these with the use of utility landing craft or helicopters. However, delays in the transfer of payments slowed down this programme by quite some. Only Hengam and Larak were completed in August and November 1974. The contract for the other two was formally cancelled in March 1979. Nevertheless, because the yard had assembled, or had on order, enough material for the last two vessels, Tehran then changed its mind and ordered their completion as 'hospital ships' named Lavan and Tonb: correspondingly, the British delivered them without any kind of armament in 1985.

Originally, the Hengam-class was to support the Marine Corps (Takavaran) of the IIN, officially established in March 1973, and largely trained by the British at a newly constructed training centre in Manjil. Within the first year, the latter turned out a class of 80 troops, and by 1975 there were enough around to establish their first company. However, subsequent growth of the Iranian Marine Corps was more significant: by 1978, two battalions were operational, as was the first squadron of the IIN's British-trained Special Boat Service (SBS).

MINE WARFARE

Despite the high sensitivity of the – generally – shallow Persian Gulf to mining operations, the IIN showed very little interest in such weapons. As far as is known, in the early 1970s the IIN had only 60 old British-made Mk 17s, and 32 US-made Mk 6 moored mines with contact fuses, all designed and manufactured during the Second World War. Whether the IIN received a small number of air-dropped Mk.56 moored magnetic mines before 1979 remains unclear.

The IIN planned to complement the four Hengams through an order for five commercial Ro-Ros – the Arya Rakhhsh-class, classified as landing ships and minelayers – constructed by the Teraoka Yard in Japan in 1978. This decision was taken shortly before the fall of the Shah, just like the acquisition of seven Delvar-class support ships constructed in Pakistan. Their story is to be told further below.[10]

REVOLUTION OF 1979

By 1979 the Iranian navy had 30,000 men, the majority conscripts, with selected men having their service extended in seven-year batches (for up to a maximum of 30 years total service before retirement). Officers were graduates either of the Ground Forces Academy or major naval educational institutions in Britain, France, West Germany and Italy. There was also a coast guard, based upon the Imperial Iranian Gendarmerie, equipped with three Gohar-class fishery protection vessels, nine Sewart-type patrol boats, and 26 US-made Patrol Boat, River (PBR) Mk II and Mk IIIs by the time of the Revolution. Subsequently, most were taken up by the Iranian navy, which held them in high esteem. These small, rigid-hulled boats were originally developed for riverine operations in Vietnam: their hull was made of fiberglass, and they had a water jet drive, which enabled them to operate in very shallow, silt- and weed-choked waters. The water jet drive also made them highly manoeuvrable: by reversing it, the boat could make a 180-degree turn in its own length, or come to a stop from full speed in only a few boat lengths. The majority of PBRs had a crew of four, and were armed with twin M2 .50-cal (12.7mm) heavy machine guns at the front, and a single M2 to the rear, and with one or two side-mounted 7.62mm M60 machine guns. All were armoured with ceramic shields fitted to their bridge and gun shields, while crews were equipped with ballistic helmets and blankets.[11]

At that point in time, the Shah was overthrown and a quasi-theocracy established itself in power that quickly antagonised the West, and especially the USA. Unsurprisingly, in March and April 1979, Washington, which had been willing to work with the new regime, quickly cancelled all military orders – at the time worth over US$10 billion – and its allies in Western Europe followed in fashion.[12] The crisis culminated in an invasion of the US Embassy in Tehran and taking of its staff hostage, and an abortive rescue operation that failed and ended in US humiliation, ruining relations between two former allies until the present day.

Although the IIN personnel could be described as 'generally supportive of the revolution', the new regime launched a major demobilisation, and the navy was no exception: over 120 of its top officers were purged by the summer of 1980. The service was renamed the Islamic Republic of Iran Navy (IRIN) and downsized to about 22,000 personnel, commanded by Captain Bahram Afzali.[13] During the first week of his tour, Afzali was busy renaming vessels, as listed in Table 5. Otherwise, he largely retained the earlier organisation into four districts, of which the 1st, 2nd and 3rd were in the Persian Gulf, and the 4th – headquartered in Bandar-e Azali – the Caspian Sea. In the Persian Gulf, the boundary between the 1st and 2nd Districts was the 28th Parallel, with the Bandar-e Abbas Fleet Command Post also controlling the island garrisons, while the 3rd District, which later moved its headquarters to Bandar-e Shahpour/Bandar-e Khomeini, was a port defence organisation. Henceforth, all officer-training was performed in country, at the main training centre in Bandar-e Anzali (which included simulators for crews of the Kaman-class FACs) – although a few cadets were also sent on courses to the Indian Navy Staff College.

3
IRAQ'S NAVAL REACTION

To a certain degree, Iraq could only look on with envy at its neighbour's naval expansion. Generally, Iraq was arming itself because of the arms race started by Iran, which was seen as a main threat, but also because of its participation in the Arab-Israeli conflict, and continuous Kurdish insurgencies in the north. Nevertheless, Iraq never seriously challenged Iran's naval superiority in the Gulf: during the 1970s the Iraqi Armed Forces underwent a massive expansion on their own but this was motivated by recent wars with Israel (in June 1967 and October 1973), and with Kurdish insurgencies in the north (1974–75) supported by Iran and the Soviet Union. Facing such threats, Baghdad had little option but to focus on bolstering its ground forces. Marred by Soviet failures to deliver equipment that the Iraqis considered advanced enough for their purposes, even the IrAF experienced a period of relatively slow qualitative growth during the mid-1970s, before Baghdad's representatives managed to conclude negotiations that had lasted for years with Paris for the acquisition of Dassault Mirage F.1 multi-role fighters. That said, the principal reason for the slow expansion of the Iraqi Navy was that the country was almost landlocked and had a very short coastline. Certainly enough, this coastline was slightly longer considering that the Shatt al-Arab marked much of the southern border of Iraq and Iran. However, geography inevitably shaped Baghdad's response. Foremost, traditionally, the Persian Gulf has enjoyed the same legal status as the 'open seas', while Iraq made substantial effort to use pipelines to the Mediterranean for its oil exports. It was only in the second half of the 1970s, once Iran began openly exercising its dominance of the Persian Gulf, that – in the light of its protests remaining fruitless – Baghdad began developing designs to counter Tehran's naval build-up.

IRAQI NAVY[1]
The Iraqi Navy was officially established on 2 July 1937 in Baghdad, as a purely riverine force. In August of the same year, its headquarters (HQ) were moved to al-Amara, where a small berth was constructed as a homeport for its first few patrol boats of local construction. Later in 1937, these were reinforced by four bigger vessels with displacement of 67 tons, constructed by Thornycroft

One of three SO-1 patrol ships of the Iraqi Navy, acquired from the USSR in 1962. Each was armed with two twin 2M-3M 25mm guns, and four RBU-1200 Uragan ASW mortars, but could also carry up to 24 depth charges or 10 mines. (Ali Altobchi collection)

The Iraqi Navy ship *Yarmouk*, seen during the handover ceremony, still wearing the Soviet Red Star and hull number – but already flying its new national flag. This was the first of two T-43-class ocean minesweepers of Soviet origin. They were armed with two twin 37mm guns and two twin 25mm guns, two projectors for depth charges, and could carry 16 mines. (Ali Altochi collection)

A decade of latent political instability was concluded with two coups in 1969, the latter of which established President (and Major General of the Iraqi Army) Ahmed Hassan al-Bakr, with his younger cousin (and civilian) Hussein Abd al-Majid at-Tikriti – nicknamed 'Saddam' – as Vice-President. Under these two, over the following 10 years Iraq experienced an unprecedented period of (almost) peace and economic growth, strongly fuelled by a campaign of nationalisation of the nation's oil- and gas industry.

The Iraqi Navy was one of the beneficiaries of this development – even more so because its top brass was quick to realise that in order to counter the Iranian naval build-up, it had to first develop its own naval educational facilities, before expanding its fleet. Correspondingly, in 1970, the Arab Gulf Academy for Sea Studies was established in Basra, to train military and naval engineering staff for Iraq, and also for allied Arab states. Amongst others, this offered a bachelor's degree in war and engineering naval sciences. Moreover, around the same time Moscow provided three Projeckt 183R Komar-class fast missile craft. Each of these 38 knot, 70 ton boats was armed with a pair of P-15 Termit anti-ship missiles (ASCC/NATO codename 'SS-N-2 Styx'), and one twin 25mm 2M-3M cannon with 1,000 rounds. The Komars seem never to have received Iraqi designations and were primarily used for training purposes, preparing the Iraqi Navy for the acquisition of more advanced vessels. In 1974, Baghdad purchased six Projekt 205 Tsunami-class FACs (ASCC/NATO codename 'Osa I') from the USSR. These 38.5m long vessels displaced 209 tons at full load, and each was equipped with four launchers for P-15s and two 30mm AK-230 automatic guns.[2]

By 1978, the Iraqi FAC fleet was reinforced by four pairs of slightly more advanced Projekt 205ER-class FACs (ASCC/NATO codename 'Osa II'). Following the training of their crews in the USSR, they entered service with the newly established 4th Naval Brigade. Around the same time, the torpedo tubes were removed from old the P-6 MTBs, which were 'downgraded' to fast patrol boats, and then reinforced through the acquisition of five Projekt-1400 Zhuk-class patrol boats, and two (unarmed) Nyrat II-class patrol craft. Moreover, the Iraqi Navy then established the 6th Naval Brigade, equipped with three Projekt-1258 Korund/Yevgenya-class inshore minesweepers while, in 1977–78, it acquired four Polnocny-D-class amphibious warfare vessels. Named *Atika*, *Jananda*, *Nouh* and *Ganda*, these were each capable of carrying six tanks or 180 troops, and supporting them with 140mm unguided rockets fired from two multiple rocket launch systems.

in Great Britain and armed with mortars and machine guns. In 1956, the HQ was transferred to the traditional merchant port of Basra, but the fleet remained the same and was long overdue for replacement. Even then, the service's status was so low, that while Baghdad went to great extents to expand the air force, the new compound of the HQ in Basra was completed only in July 1960. The Iraqi Navy did eventually profit from establishment of better relations with the USSR following the Tammuz Revolution of 1958, and on 27 November 1959 received its first three Soviet-made P-6 motor torpedo boats. Three additional vessels of the same class followed by 1962, and this fleet received the hull numbers 217 to 222. In 1962, the Iraqi Navy received its biggest warships up to that point: three Projekt 201 SO-1-class patrol boats, which received hull designations 310, 311, and 312.

Amid continuous political turbulence that marred the country, in 1966 the force was redesignated as the Navy and Coast Defence Headquarters, and was bolstered not only by the acquisition of a regiment-worth of 130mm coastal defence guns, but also the work of an Egyptian training mission, which provided valuable experience. However, a year later, the June 1967 Arab-Israeli War was fought, which prompted Baghdad into another expansion of its army and air force. Thus, there was too little funding left available for its diminutive navy. Over the following years, this was bolstered through the acquisition of more than two Poluchat I-class coastal patrol craft with displacement of 90 tons at full load, and two 580-ton T-43-class ocean minesweepers of Soviet origin: the latter two were named *Yarmouk* (465) and *al-Kadisia* (467).

An Iraqi P-6 motor torpedo boat at high speed. Once the Osa Is and Osa IIs became operational, the Iraqis removed the torpedo tubes from the P-6s and relegated them to patrol duties. (Ali Altobchi collection)

A still from a video showing an Iraqi Projekt-205-class (Osa) FAC at high speed, probably underway on the Khowr az-Zubayr River, on the approaches to the navy's new main base in Umm Qasr. (Ivan Zajac collection)

A Zhuk-class patrol boat (hull number 109), five of which were acquired starting in 1975. Displacing 39 tons, they were armed with two twin 12.7mm machine guns and deployed for security purposes only. (Ali Altobchi collection)

Finally, because Basra was within artillery range of the Iranian border, a new naval base was established near the Kuwaiti border on the Khowr az-Zubayr River, at Umm Qasr, and most of the Iraqi warships moved there during the late 1970s. Elsewhere, the service had very few contacts abroad and courtesy visits were rare: the few that took place were largely confined to the ports on the western side of the Persian Gulf. Nevertheless, in April 1978, three Iraqi warships paid a visit to Aden, in the People's Democratic Republic of Yemen (colloquially 'South Yemen').

FINAL EXPANSION

While the further development of the Iranian navy all but stopped in February 1979, that of the Iraqi Navy intensified. Keen to obtain a blue water capability, in 1978 Saddam Hussein – who was already on the way to establish himself in power in Baghdad – approached France and Italy with a request for help with improving training. Apparently, nothing happened until he actually assumed power in June 1979, when Saddam turned to Yugoslavia instead. In a matter of a few months, he acquired a training frigate displacing 1,850 tons. Named *Ibn Khaldum*, and accompanied by the salvage ship *Akka* (also from Yugoslavia) this arrived in the spring of 1980, and – at least officially – became the flagship of the Iraqi Navy's 7th Naval Brigade: *Ibn Khaldum* was soon renamed *Ibn Marjid* and was primarily deployed for transport purposes. A few weeks later, three Neštin-class river minesweepers were acquired from Yugoslavia while Saddam entered negotiations with Moscow for the acquisition of additional FACs.

Through the next few months, the new Iraqi dictator was busy fighting the war with Iran, but his representatives in Europe were not sitting idle: on

GORSHKOV'S MISSILE REVOLUTION

The Iran-Iraq War was to see the most extensive use of the newest weapon in the naval armoury: the guided anti-ship missile. Rocket-powered, air-launched weapons were developed and used during the Second World War. While a few Western navies did experiment with installing cruise missiles on their vessels, they proved less enthusiastic about developing anti-ship weapons in that category. During the mid-1950s, the Soviets came to a different conclusion: in 1956, the Kremlin appointed Admiral Sergei Georglyevich Gorshkov as the new commander-in-chief of the Soviet Navy, with the task of reforming the service and make it capable of defending the USSR from attacks by US Navy aircraft carriers. Gorshkov completely revamped the navy: he scrapped older, Russian-built ships, war prizes, and all the battleships – about 300 ships were stricken in his purge – and replaced them with a large number of small and fast missile boats, armed with heavy anti-ship missiles. Even once he ordered the construction of heavier vessels in the early 1960s, the first to come out were the Kynda-class cruisers that shocked the naval community in the West by being the first major warships with a main battery entirely consisting of anti-ship missiles.

Obviously, Gorshkov's reform of the Soviet Navy resulted in the emergence of a number of anti-ship missiles. The type that saw the most widespread deployment was the active radar homing, rocket propelled weapon designated the P-15 or Termit. It was a hefty missile, weighing more than 2,000kg on launch, of which no less than 513kg belonged to a hollow-charge, high-explosive warhead. Given the ASCC/NATO reporting name 'SS-N-2 Styx', and having a range of more than 20nm (about 40km), it posed a serious threat to the Western navies' major surface combatants and became the primary armament of missile boats. The P-15 was widely exported in the 1970s, and although its corrosive fuel created major maintenance problems it was a system that was simple to operate. It proved effective in combat and could be pre-programmed to approach its target at Mach 0.9 at altitudes of 25, 50, or 250 metres.

While developing air defence systems – like Tartar/Terrier and Standard in the USA, or Seaslug and Sea Dart in Great Britain – the West largely continued ignoring anti-ship missiles. One exception to this rule was Sweden where Saab and the French company Nord Aviation (later Aérospatiale) developed an anti-ship version of the CT-20 target drone, designated the Rb (Robot) 08. This was installed on destroyers of the Swedish Navy starting from 1955. The same year Aérospatiale began exploiting their expertise to produce subsonic ship-launched anti-ship missiles with the project definition that would ultimately become Exocet (Flying Fish). The only other Western navies interested in this technology were Italy and Norway. In 1960, the latter decided to produce a fleet of FACs equipped with a weapon the development of which began a year later, and which eventually became the Penguin missile. Italy launched its Project Nettuno in 1963, as a beam-riding weapon, and two years later Contraves Italiana launched Project Vulcano, with a similar guidance system. Only the latter reached the trial phase, but never entered production. In 1967, the Italian Sistel consortium of five major companies then joined their efforts: the work on Nettuno and Vulcano was completed and they entered production under the designations Sea Killer Mk. 1 and Mk. 2. The Sea Killer Mk. 2 was purchased by Iran for its frigates constructed by Vosper, but failed to attract other customers: nevertheless, development continued in the form of a helicopter-launched weapon named Marte. Meanwhile, after becoming the first navy to lose a major combatant to an anti-ship missile – the destroyer INS *Eilat*, sunk by Styx missiles launched from Egyptian-operated fast missile craft, in October 1967 – Israel launched the development of its Gabriel missile.

The sinking of *Eilat* shocked Western navies and stimulated development of the rocket-powered Exocet – first as the ship-launched MM.38, and then as the air-launched AM.39. The US Navy followed in fashion with the development of an air-launched, turbojet-powered subsonic weapon named Harpoon and hastily sought a ship-launched version for its major surface combatants. The *Eilat* incident also stimulated interest among Third World

A Projekt-205ER (Osa II) boat, widely exported around the world in the 1970s. (US DoD)

navies in FACs and while those with good relations with Moscow quickly purchased dozens of small but heavily armed vessels, the allies of the West rushed to place orders with the German yard Friedrich Lürssen and CMN for vessels armed with Exocets, and electronics either made by Signaal or Thomson-CSF. This is how most of navies in the Persian Gulf came to acquire FACs, during the mid-1970s, too.

The effects of the boosters of this P-15 Termit missile, climbing from the Indian Navy missile boat Chamak (K95) during an exercise, are clearly visible here. Following in the footsteps of the Egyptian Navy, the Indian Navy was the second to deploy P-15s in combat, during the 1971 War with Pakistan. (Indian Navy Photo)

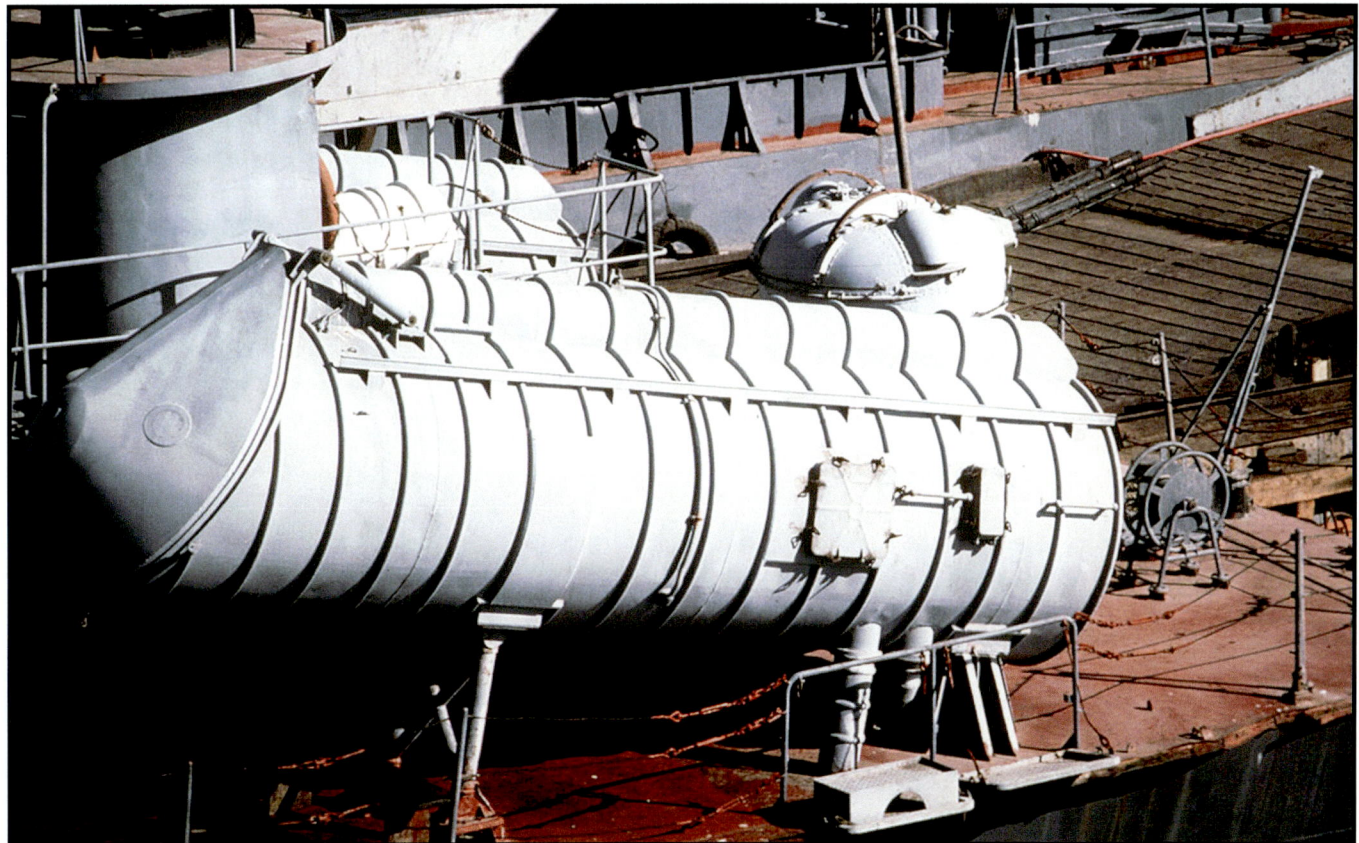
A KT-97M launcher of a Projekt-205ER-class fast missile craft (Osa II). This model could fire either the original P-15, or one of its more advanced P-20 or P-21 variants. Notable, to the rear, is one of the vessel's two turrets with twin water-cooled AKM-230 30mm guns. (US DoD)

The Neštin-class minesweepers were designed by the Naval Institute of the Yugoslav Navy for mine-clearing duties on rivers, and constructed by the Brodotehnika Shipyard in Belgrade. Each was armed with one twin- and one single-barrel 20mm gun, and one launcher for SA-7 MANPADs. They could also load 18 type AIM-M82 non-contact mines or 24 R-1 anchor mines. (via Ali Altobchi)

4 March 1981, they concluded a contract estimated at US$1.8 to 2.4 billion with Italian shipyard Cantieri Navali Riuniti for four frigates, six corvettes, an underway replenishment ship, and a floating dock.[3] Combined with the acquisition of Polnocny-D amphibious warfare vessels, this acquisition obviously aimed not only to match the Iranian naval power, but probably to – sooner, rather than later – help secure the Tunbs and Abu Musa, and also Kuwait's Bubiyan and Warbah Islands.

The four 2,525-ton Lupo-class frigates had Italian RAN-10/11 search- and RTN-10/20 weapon control radars, US-made Edo 610 or Raytheon 1160 sonars, Otomat Mk II anti-ship missiles and Albatros SAMs, a 127mm gun, two lightweight torpedo launchers, and enough deck and hangar space for two helicopters. Named *Hittin*, *Thi Quar*, *Al Qadissiya* and *Al Yarmouk*, they were launched between 1983 and 1985 but completion was delayed because of US objections to their use of LM 2500 gas turbines in the CODOG propulsion system. Scheduled to re-form the 4th Naval Brigade, they were completed between 1985 and 1987, and a token party of Iraqi sailors manned them. However, due to the UN arms embargo – and, even more importantly: the sheer impossibility of them safely reaching any Iraqi port – none was ever delivered: although released in 1990, they were promptly embargoed again because of Iraq's invasion of Kuwait. Eventually, all were purchased by the Italian Navy instead.

The six 675-ton corvettes were named the Abi Serh-class and planned to form the 7th Naval Brigade. Four – named *Abdullah Ibn Abi Serh*, *Kalid Ibn al-Walid*, *Saad Ibn Abi Wakkad*, and *Salah Aldin Ayoobi* – were based upon the Wadi Mragh-class, constructed for Libya, while *Musa Ben Nussair* and *Tariq Ibn Ziyad* were based upon the Ecuadorian Esmeralda-class, with reduced SAM systems but retained a helicopter landing pad. Ultimately, their fate was similar to that of the Lupos: all were sold to foreign navies in the late 1990s. Only slightly different was the fate of the 9,100-ton Stromboli-class replenishment ship *Agnadeen*: this was commissioned in 1984, and had reached the port of Alexandria in Egypt, but was then stopped and still around at least as of 2013.

AIR SUPPORT

Unlike Iran, Iraq was slow in providing its navy with air support: indeed, no naval aviation branch was ever officially established. Having just experienced two bitter wars, for most of the mid-1970s the Iraqi Air Force was preoccupied with finding a solution to facing two technologically superior threats – Israel in the west, and Iran in the east – and the permanent menace in the form of Kurdish insurgencies in the north, rather than thinking about the possible need to support the navy, sometime in the future.[4]

Furthermore, although Saddam Hussein was fascinated by the F-14 Tomcat acquired by Iran, Iraq lacked contacts and sources for similar technology – at least until closer ties were established with France in late 1974, and Paris offered Mirages to Iraq. Although Saddam, then still in the function of a Vice-President, reached the decision to purchase this fighter-bomber by November 1975, the IrAF was sceptical, and – depending on the individuals' professional background – its leadership preferred either the US-made F-4 Phantom, or the Soviet-made Sukhoi Su-20/22 fighter-bombers. Moreover, much of the equipment and weaponry the French Ministerial Delegation for Armament (*Délégation Ministérielle pour l'Armement*, DMA), and its subdivision Direction of International Affairs (*Direction des Affaires Internationales*, DIA), were offering to Iraq were still just the ideas of designers working for different enterprises; a few were on the 'drawing boards', but very little was already undergoing research and development, and even less so in production. Paris lacked money to finance the related work. Nevertheless, the generals of the IrAF agreed to acquire the small fighter-bomber on condition of the French delivering their best available high-technologies and latest weaponry, together with full transfer of the related know-how. Indeed, in several cases they demanded the development of entirely new weapons systems for their Mirages. By the time all the details were sorted out and put on paper, and the contract for the resulting Project Baz signed, it was already early July 1977. From that point onwards, the French expected that it would take them three years to start deliveries.

That said, in late 1975 Baghdad opted to place a huge order for French-made helicopters armed with the latest guided missiles. Amongst these were 16 Aérospatiale SA.321 Super Frelon Helicopters and 60 of the latest Aérospatiale AM.39 Exocet anti-ship missiles – all of which were ordered on the insistence of the

Table 6: Aérospatiale SA.321GV Super Frelon Helicopters of Iraq			
Construction Number	Delivered	IrAF Serial Number	Note
177	15 August 1976		written off 1 August 1983
180	15 August 1976		written off 1 November 1976
181	3 February 1977		
183	23 June 1976		
184	23 June 1976		written off 6 February 1979
186	3 February 1977		impounded in France 1990
187	25 September 1977		written off 1 June 1987
188	3 February 1977	2024	impounded in France 1990
189	25 September 1977		written off 4 August 1981
190	25 September 1977		
191	16 October 1977		
192	16 October 1977		
196	17 July 1980	2021	written off 16 January 1987
197	27 July 1980	2022	written off 1 August 1984

the most advanced avionics the USSR had to offer at the time (including a Doppler speed and drift sensor, compatibility with Kh-23E radio-command guided missiles, and KKR-1 reconnaissance pods), the Su-22 proved a disappointment for the leadership of the IrAF. The delivery of 'under-equipped' Sukhois significantly contributed to the Iraqi decision to stop purchasing Soviet fighter-bombers and to start buying French instead. It was only in late 1978, when Major Hisham Ismail Barbouti – an enterprising MiG-23 pilot – was assigned the command of No. 109 Squadron, that this unit actually started training in anti-ship operations.[7]

contemporary staff of the Iraqi Navy, which wished to benefit from cooperation with the IrAF.

Officially at least, the first nine Super Frelons were all completed to the relatively simple SA.321H variant, primarily equipped for search and rescue purposes, and with a secondary anti-submarine capability. Actually, all 16 were completed to the SA.321GV standard: based on the SA.321GB anti-submarine version developed for the *Marine nationale*, they retained the ASW capability and the Omera-Segid/Thomson-CSF ORB.31D Héraclés-1 surveillance and fire-control radar installed in a prominent fairing on the nose of the helicopter. Indeed, the last few examples manufactured for Iraq were equipped with an even more advanced fire-control system, centred on the ORB.32W Héraclés-2 radar: this had its main antenna installed inside the same housing on the nose as the ORB.31-equipped examples, along with additional aerials installed on the floats.[5]

The training of crews drawn from the IrAF was carried out entirely in France and began in 1976, while the installation of Exocets and related testing was initiated a year later: eventually, a total of 14 Super Frelons were handed over to Iraqi representatives in France between 15 August 1976 and 16 October 1977. The first of them were transferred to Baghdad on board newly acquired Ilyushin Il-76MD transport aircraft of the IrAF in 1978. Once there, they entered service with the newly established No. 101 Squadron, homebased at Wahda AB (formerly RAF Shoibiyah), 45km south-west of Basra. With this, the unit was relatively close to the navy's main base in Umm Qasr, and thus the junior service had at least some hope of receiving support from the Super Frelons, even if lacking administrative control over them. This changed in the summer of 1980, when the IrAF was reorganised and the mass of its helicopter fleet handed over to the newly established Iraqi Army Aviation Corps (IrAAC). In the course of the same reform, No. 101 Squadron was officially reassigned to the Iraqi Navy.[6]

Other than handing out this single helicopter squadron, the IrAF limited its activities in support of the navy. Arguably, when it acquired 36 big and powerful Sukhoi Su-22 fighter-bombers in 1976–77, it deployed one of two units operating them – No. 109 Squadron – to Wahda AB. However, even if outfitted with some of

IRAQI NAVY OF 1980

In conclusion, it can be said that as of 1980, both the Iraqi Navy and the Iraqi Air Force were mid-way through another expansion and partial re-equipment with custom-made armament of Western origin, but still years away from actually receiving these. Indeed, the navy – at the time commanded by Lieutenant General Aladdin Hammad al-Janabi (sometimes described as an 'utter vasal of the regime') – was still a small force of between 3,000 and 4,250 men, with most ratings being volunteers on five-year enlistments, and most officers graduates of Egyptian, Indian, Pakistani, and Yugoslav educational facilities, or courses provided by foreign instructors. Although Iraq was widely misdescribed as a sort of 'Soviet puppet' or at least a 'Soviet ally' in the West, Moscow's capability to influence Baghdad was non-existent, and the Soviet presence and involvement were minimal: the USSR was providing conversion training only, and significant amounts of logistical support, but this was always tied to the quality of relations between Baghdad and Moscow – which sored through the late 1970s.

The navy's main storage facility remained the Dhat as-Sawari Naval Base in Basra, but the service was plagued by shortages of spares, even if technical services proved capable of running routine maintenance: whenever not, commercial companies were contracted to conduct refits. As a result, the old SO-1s, T-43s, and more recent Osas were reported as well-maintained, but the condition of P-6s was not as good. Perhaps more importantly, while most of the fleet was based at Umm Qasr, two of the Polnocnys – *Ganda* and *Jananda* – were undergoing repairs in a yard on the Shatt al-Arab as of September 1980, and were to remain 'locked' there for the duration of the war with Iran: at most, the Iraqis were able to make use of their multiple rocket launchers.

The new base in Umm Qasr had a dry dock and extensive facilities, which were well-protected from air strikes, but on the al-Faw Peninsula, the southernmost tip of Iraq, the navy could do little other than make use of local commercial facilities. Perhaps more importantly, the Iraqi Navy acquired three French-made TRS.3004 Sea Tiger E/F-band coastal surveillance radars and deployed them in the al-Faw area: these had a nominal detection range of around 60–80 kilometres (depending on weather conditions) and were used to support 130mm guns operated by coastal defence battalions. Moreover, the navy was in the process of acquiring two batteries of Chinese-made HY-2 anti-ship missiles: essentially a coastal-defence variant of the Soviet-made P-15, and they were to reach the Faw Peninsula in 1982.

Overall, the Iraqi seamen were well-trained and could make good use of their equipment. However – and contrary to the IrAF – they had no electronic warfare equipment whatsoever, and were woefully short on operational experience. For example, while loyal to Saddam, Janabi was a former commander of a naval infantry battalion, and his subordinates were no better in this regard. Moreover, the Iraqi Navy was ill-positioned to contribute to Saddam's plan for the invasion of Iran.

4
CRISIS AND ESCALATION

When Mohammed Reza Shah Pahlavi of Iran was toppled by what subsequently became known as the 'Islamic' Revolution, and a quasi-clerical regime took over in February 1979, Iraq sought an accommodation with the new authorities in Tehran. To no avail. Not only was the new Iranian leader, Ayatollah Sayyid Ruhollah Musavi Khomeini, longing to 'avenge' his deportation from exile in Iraq in 1978: soon after establishing himself in power, Saddam ordered the arrest and then the execution of one of Iraq's leading Shi'a clerics and Khomeini's allies, Muhammad Baqir as-Sadr. Khomeini reacted by broadcasting calls for an Islamic revolution in Iraq and overthrow of the regime in Baghdad. Thus began a crisis that was to lead to the longest conventional war in the second half of the twentieth century.

IGNORED WARNINGS[1]
Enmities between Persians (predominantly members of the Shi'a branch of Islam) and Arabs (most of whom are members of the Sunni branch) are centuries old, but mutual wars relatively rare. Iraq is the site of major holy places of the Shi'a, and over centuries dozens of thousands of Persians have settled around the two principal ones – Najaf and Karbala: although coming under the control of local authorities during the times of the – predominantly Sunni – Ottoman Empire, they have never integrated in language, custom, residence and nationality with Iraq. Unsurprisingly, the British during the 1920s, but especially a government like the one established by Saddam Hussein of 1979, have always considered them a sort of 'fifth column'. On the other hand, most of Iran never contained any large concentrations of Arabs except in its southwestern Khuzestan province, which did retain a large Arab minority. These Arabs did not identify with Iraq, and – generally – have conducted themselves as loyal Iranian subjects, until the times of the revolution of 1978–79, when the new regime began questioning their loyalty. Saddam and Khomeini were already at odds before the latter established himself in power in 1979, and through that year their mutual threats – usually expressed in the media they controlled – were replaced by politically-motivated violence as both sides began providing material and financial support to each other's dissidents. Arguably, during the 6th Summit of Non-Aligned Movement, held in Havana, the capital of Cuba, between 3 and 9 September 1979, Saddam Hussein met the Iranian Minister of Foreign Affairs, Ebrahim Yazdi, and the two reached an agreement to end all such activities. However, the Iranian intelligence and security service SAVAMA managed to 'bug' the compound of the Iraqi delegation.[2] This is how it came to be that the Iranians recorded a chat between Saddam and his aide Salah Omar al-Ali, one of the top members of the Iraqi Ba'ath Party. When al-Ali observed that he was very happy with the outcome of negotiations with the Iranians, and hoping the crisis was over, Saddam answered bluntly:

Do you know what is diplomacy? What has spoiled your mind? What peace? What problems solved between us and Iran? This, Sallah, is the chance that may happen once in a century. Right now we have the chance while their country is split and their armed forces falling apart. It is our historical chance to regain our rights...

Of course, SAVAMA forwarded the resulting warnings all the way up the chain of command in Tehran: however, preoccupied with fighting the civil war against multiple opponents in the country, and mistrusting the 'Shah's intelligence', Khomeini and his aides ignored them. In October 1979, units of the Iraqi Navy and its 77th Naval Infantry Brigade then held an exercise simulating an invasion of the Tunb Islands and Abu Mussa. Once again, this did not escape the attention of SAVAMA: a corresponding report was filed and forwarded up the chain of command in Tehran. Once again, Khomeini and his aides preferred to ignore it. The top ranks of the Iranian armed forces did not: on 22 November 1979, the Joint Chiefs of Staff of the Armed Forces of the Islamic Republic of Iran (JCS) held a conference with the Commanders and Deputy Commanders for Operations of all IRIAF air bases. The meeting resulted in the conclusion that the air force should be prepared for the event of a surprise Iraqi attack, and promptly retaliate with air strikes on IrAF air bases. Correspondingly, on 1 December 1979, the JCS issued a set of orders designated Plan Entegham to major IRIAF units – in the event of a sudden Iraqi invasion:

- TFB.1 (Mehrabad, Tehran): to strike Taqaddum AB (west of Baghdad, and north of the former RAF Habbaniya) and Muthanna AB (northern Baghdad);
- TFB.2 (Tabriz): to strike Kirkuk and Mosul air bases and nearby radar stations;
- TFB.3 (Hamedan): to strike Rashid AB (Baghdad), the old Habbaniya AB, al-Kut AB, and radar stations named an-Naji and ar-Rashid;
- TFB.4 (Dezful): to strike Ali Ibn Abu Talib AB (an-Nasiriyah) and its radar station, and the radar station outside al-Qut;
- TFB.6 (Bushehr): to strike Shoibiyah AB and its radar station, and Umm Qasr naval base;
- TFB.8 (Esfahan): to prepare its F-14 to act as airborne early warning assets and provide top cover for other units active in the operational area;
- TFB.9 (Bandar-e Abbas): to prepare for supporting naval operations in the Hormuz Straits and western Persian Gulf.

Later the same month, the JCS went a step further and developed Plan Abouzar, the essence of which was a number of directives detailing measures to be taken by all major units of the armed forces in the case of an Iraqi surprise attack. Sadly, precise details of Plan Abouzar are known for only three cases, all related to the army (Plan Davood, for the 28th Division; Plan Horr, for the 81st Armoured Division, and the one prepared for the 92nd Armoured Division). As far as is known, the Islamic Republic of Iran Naval Aviation (IRINA) reacted by drafting its own contingency plan; Plan Shahin. By the spring of 1980, this was reworked as Plan Zolfaghar, which envisaged six cases, including:

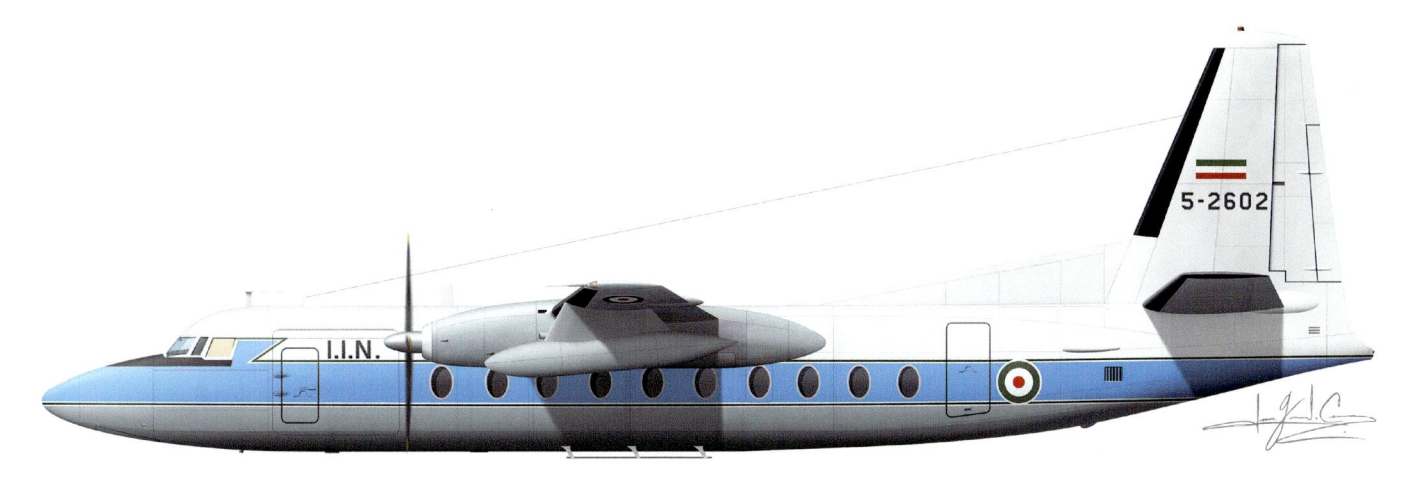

Purposely designed to replace the venerable Douglas DC-3 as a medium transport, the Fokker F.27 made its first flight in 1955 and proved highly popular and a great commercial success. Following in the footsteps of the IIAF, which acquired a total of 12 starting in 1972, the IINA acquired four for liaison and tactical airlift. Two of these were F.27-400M Troopships (equipped for troops or cargo and with wider doors in the rear), and two were F.27-600 Friendships (passenger variant). This F.27-600 is shown in the livery and markings worn immediately on delivery and for a relatively short period of time in late 1975: with upper fuselage surfaces in white, two cheat lines in dark green and one in light blue, the lower sides of the fuselage, and the wing all in gull gray. (Artwork by Luca Canossa)

With the IRIN always closely following the latest patterns in the development of camouflage colours, by 1977 all four of its F.27s were repainted in mid-grey overall. The service crest and title were applied below the cockpit, and the serial repeated on the fin. Corresponding to the system introduced in January 1976, the latter consisted of five digits: serial numbers 5-2601 and 5-2603 were applied on two F.27-600 Friendships, while serial numbers 5-2602 and 5-2604 on two F.27-400M Troopships. Later on, following locally undertaken overhauls, all four had the same camouflage pattern as the P-3Fs. (Artwork by Luca Canossa)

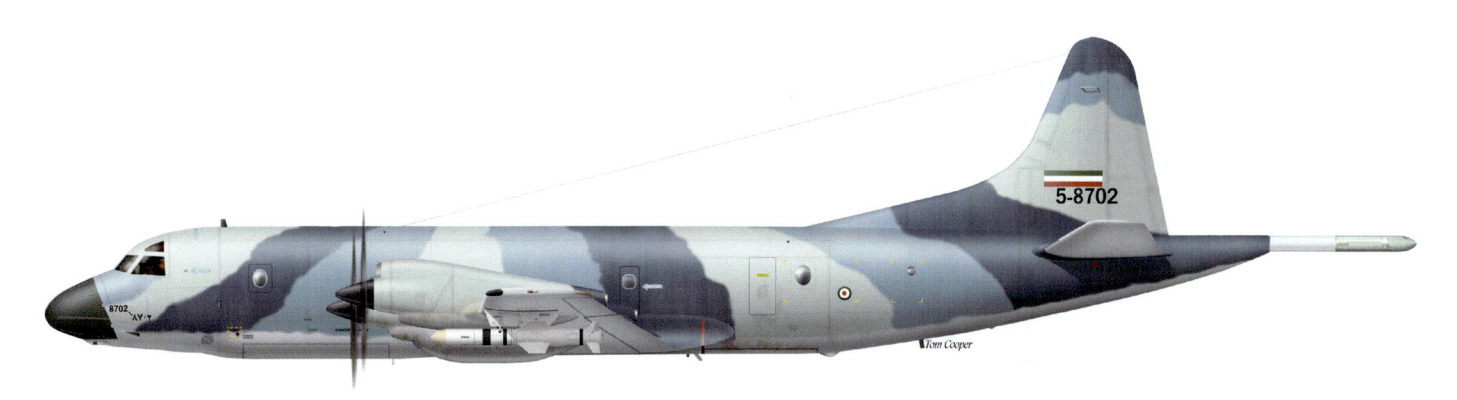

The six Lockheed P-3F Orions destined for Iran were originally taken from surplus stocks of the USN and thus prepared for delivery to Iran while still wearing white on top of the fuselage and the fin, and gull gray on undersurfaces and the wing. This was complemented with IIAF service titles and four-digit serials from 5-256 to 5-261. Shortly before their delivery, the Iranians requested their repainting in an attractive tactical three-tone camouflage pattern consisting of azure blue, dark grey, and sky, with a – deliberate – matt finish. Effective from 1 January 1976, their serial numbers were expanded to five digits, from 5-8701 to 5-8706. Two years later, this example was sent to the USA for trial installation of the then brand-new AGM-84A Harpoon anti-ship missile: a maximum of four of these could be carried on four underwing pylons. The aircraft and the first batch of Harpoons were returned to Iran, but the rest of that order (and the order for additional P-3Fs) was cancelled in March–April 1979. (Artwork by Tom Cooper)

Iran acquired a total of 20 Agusta-Bell AB.212ASW helicopters. Originally intended for deployment from destroyers such as *Babr* and *Palang*, they proved highly versatile: all were equipped with inflatable floats (installed on outriggers for their skis), and a sight for anti-tank guided missiles. In addition to their ASW role, they were deployed for search and rescue, deploying commandos of the Iranian SBS, and for ground attack. All were painted in medium sea grey overall, but most originally had their cockpit doors and fins painted in dayglo orange. Always applied in white, their serials were in the range 6-2401 to 6-2420, and the last three digits were always repeated on the boom. (Artwork by Luca Canossa)

The AB.212ASW was compatible with a wide range of weaponry. Foremost among these were Mk. 44AS and Mk. 46 lightweight torpedoes, and depth charges. In addition to Mk. 46s, Iran acquired GPU-2/A gun pods with a six-barrel 20mm automatic cannon, LAU-3A and AEREA HL-12-70 pods for 68mm unguided rockets, and French-made AS.12 anti-tank guided missiles (illustrated here), for which most of them received a sight housed inside a grey box atop the left side of the cockpit. Bar the torpedoes, all of these weapons were regularly deployed by IRINA AB.212ASWs during the war with Iraq. The helicopter illustrated here was crewed by Captain Askar Mohtaj and co-pilot 1st Lieutenant Azizi, when ordered to attack two Iraqi missile boats that seized a PBR of the IRIN in the Shatt al-Arab on 20 September 1980. The crew scored at least one hit with an AS.12, disabling one of the Iraqi vessels, but in turn collided with high tension wires and crashed. (Artwork by Luca Canossa)

Iran originally acquired seven Sikorsky RH-53D Sea Stallion helicopters, intending to deploy them for minesweeping purposes with use of Edo Mk.105 hydrofoil anti-magnetic mine vehicles, released through the rear loading ramp and towed through the water astern of the helicopter. Alternatively, they could carry at last 37 fully armed troops on fold-down wall seats, or 24 stretcher casualties and four attendants, or 8,000lbs (3629kg) of cargo. All were painted as shown here, in white on the upper half, and gull gray underneath. Their serials were in the range 9-2701 to 9-2707 (the only known US serials are 65-412 for 9-2701, illustrated here, and 65-413 for 9-2702). During the failed hostage rescue attempt of April 1980, the US armed forces abandoned three intact RH-53Ds in Iran: one of these was destroyed in an air strike by the IRIAF, while the other two were recovered and one of them refurbished and pressed into service as 9-2708. (Artwork by Luca Canossa)

The 20 Agusta-Sikorsky helicopters acquired by the IINA were originally designated AS.61A-4 by the manufacturer, but always called the ASH-3D or SH-3D by the user. The first batch of 14 (serial numbers 8-2301 to 8-2314) were multi-role helicopters, configured for ASW as well as for SAR, or carrying troops or freight. All were equipped with the nose-mounted search radar and undernose Doppler. Most were delivered in the same dark blue-grey overall colour (with the nose and tailfin in dayglo orange) as used by the Italian Navy. Iranian Naval Aviation Sea Kings always wore quite colourful markings, including a full set of maintenance and warning insignia, the crest of the IINA (later IRINA), the service title, the 'last three' of their serial number on the rear of the cabin, and the full serial on the boom. The sole Sea King involved in Operation Morvarid – serial number 8-2308 – was still wearing this camouflage pattern (including dayglo orange) on 29 November 1980. (Artwork by Tom Cooper)

The second batch of Italian-manufactured ASH-3Ds for Iran – serial numbers 8-2314 to 8-2320 – remained multi-role helicopters and retained their AQS-18 dipping sonar with 360° search capability, the undernose Doppler, and the hoisting winch on the right side of the fuselage: instead of the nose-mounted search radar they had the AN/APS-705 targeting and missile command radar for Marte Mk 2 anti-ship missiles. Unlike the upgraded ASH-3Ds and ASH-3Hs made for the Italian and Peruvian navies, this was installed in a housing under the rear of the cabin. A Marte Mk. 2s is shown inset, for reference purposes, though Iran never received any such weapons: only in the 1990s did the IRINA acquire a batch of their Chinese copies. Sea Kings of this second batch were delivered wearing the classic camouflage pattern of the US Navy: white on the top and sides and gull gray on the undersides. Correspondingly, their maintenance stencils and serials were applied in black – as was the new service title, introduced in 1979. (Artwork by Tom Cooper)

Sometime in 1980, a number of Iranian ASH-3Ds – including serial numbers 8-2309, 8-2310, 8-2312, and 8-2313 – were overpainted in the same blue-grey colour as worn by AB.212ASWs. 8-2310, had its service title and serial number applied in white; 8-2309 had a combination of the 'last three' of its serial in black and service titles in white, and the other two had all such markings in black. All wore the full set of maintenance and warning stencils in white. Thanks to extensive maintenance facilities constructed in the 1970s, and large stocks of spare parts, the fleet was maintained in good condition and deployed very intensively during the war with Iraq. Following the cancellation of the contract for delivery of Marte Mk. 2s, Iranian Sea Kings lacked weapons for anti-surface operations, and their ASW capability was never required because Iraq had no submarines. However, they served in reconnaissance, search and rescue, and troop transport roles. (Artwork for Tom Cooper)

Officially, between 1971 and 1978, Iran acquired a total of 177 McDonnell-Douglas F-4E Phantom II fighter-bombers (in addition to 32 F-4Ds and 12 RF-4Es). By 1978, all were brought up to the so-called Mod. 556 standard, including leading edge slats for improved manoeuvrability, but only the last 32 received the TISEO telescopic TV-camera sight. This example – US-serial number 71-1115 – belonged to the second batch of 73 F-4Es, delivered between 1974 and 1976. Originally, it received the IIAF serial number 3-686, which in January 1976 was changed to 3-6552, and in 1978 to 3-6551. The aircraft is shown in the markings of TFB.6, recognisable by the Persian number 6 in a black circle, applied on the fin. It is illustrated as armed with AGM-65A Maverick electro-optically guided air-to-ground missiles, and – in the rear wells, under the engines – AIM-7E-2 Sparrow semi-active radar homing, medium-range air-to-air missiles. This jet is known to have been involved in Operation Morvarid. (Artwork by Tom Cooper)

When the IIAF was 'reorganised' as the IRIAF, very little of the look of its aircraft changed. Phantoms retained their standardised Asia Minor camouflage pattern, applied prior to delivery and specified as consisting of tan (FS30400), dark brown (FS30140), and dark green (FS34079) on upper surfaces and sides, and light gray (FS36622) on undersurfaces. Serial numbers were left in their place, and still applied in black, but service titles were expanded to IRIAF. The main difference was that the fin flash received the so-called 'onion': four crescents and a sword standing for the word 'Allah' and symbolising the five pillars of Islam, with a tashdid (used to double a letter in Arabic: here it 'doubled the strength of the sword'). This TISEO-equipped F-4E – US-serial number 73-1551, IRIAF serial number 3-6629 – was one of the last 32 Phantoms delivered to Iran. Originally, it was assigned to TFB.9, but by November 1980 it served with TFB.6, and thus became involved in Operation Morvarid, armed with a pair each of AIM-9J Sidewinders (underwing stations) and AIM-7E-2 Sparrows (in bays underneath the engines). (Artwork by Tom Cooper)

Iran acquired a total of 80 Grumman F-14A Tomcat interceptors, 79 of which were delivered between 1976 and 1978, together with 484 AIM-54A Phoenix long-range missiles (the balance of the order for AIM-54As, and a follow-up order for 75 re-engined F-14As were cancelled in April 1979). They were distributed between 72nd and 73rd TFS based at TFB.7 (Shiraz) and 81st, 82nd, and 83rd TFS at TFB.8 (Esfahan). Iranian Tomcats never received the improved AIM-9H Sidewinder and AIM-7F Sparrow missiles as planned, and fought the first months of the war with Iraq as illustrated here: with their internal M61A1 Vulcan 20mm automatic cannon and AIM-54A Phoenix missiles only. The entire fleet wore a modification of the Asia Minor camouflage pattern in tan (FS30400), dark brown (FS30140), and dark green (FS34079) on upper surfaces and sides, and light gray (FS36622) on undersurfaces, but had the front half of their radomes painted in radome tan and a large black anti-glare panel in front of the cockpit. This example – BuNo. 160334, IRIAF serial number 3-6036 – was piloted by Captain Jalal Zandi on 29 November 1980. (Artwork by Tom Cooper)

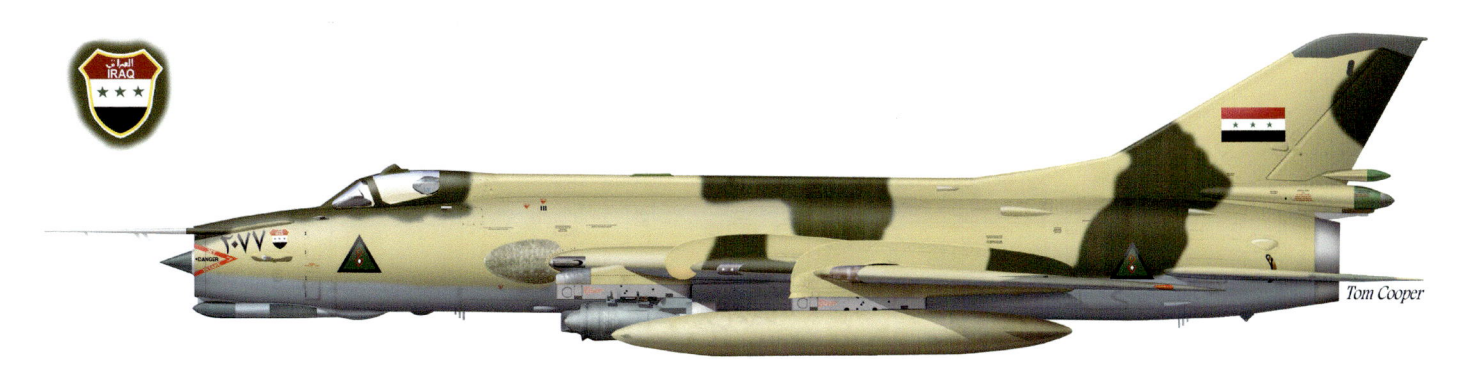

The Su-22 was an export variant of the Sukhoi Su-17, developed in response to an Iraqi demand, and equipped with a lengthened fuselage with narrower intake in comparison to the earlier Su-20, a housing with DISS-7 Doppler speed- and drift angle system under the intake, a Fon laser rangefinder and the more powerful R-29 engine. Iraq purchased a total of 36 and distributed them evenly between No. 44 Squadron and No. 109 Squadron. Sadly, the appearance of jets assigned to the latter squadron – which was the only IrAF unit trained in attacking naval targets as of 1980 – remains unknown. This example was operated by No. 44 Squadron and wore the same camouflage pattern as Su-20s, including beige (BS381C/388) and olive drab (BS381C/298) on upper surfaces and sides, and light admiralty grey (BS381C/697) on undersurfaces. Notable are an additional national marking on the forward fuselage, a mark for excellent performance in the form of a shield in Iraqi colours and the word 'Iraq' in English and Arabic, and the serial 2077. (Artwork by Tom Cooper)

In summer 1980, No. 109 Squadron at Wahda AB was reinforced through the deployment of at least one flight of four MiG-23MS from No. 39 Squadron. This early variant was 'nothing but trouble', taking IrAF four years of additional studies, flight testing, and the writing of new flight and technical manuals before it became fully operational. Even then, it suffered from poor manufacturing quality, poor navigation-attack equipment and armament. It was slated for ground attack purposes during preparations for the invasion of Iran, pending service entry of the much improved MiG-23MF. All Iraqi MiG-23MSs wore this standardised camouflage pattern consisting of beige (BS381C/388), dark brown (BS381C/411), and olive drab (BS381/298) on top surfaces and sides, and light admiralty grey (BS381C/697) on undersurfaces. (Artwork by Tom Cooper)

While probably ordering 16–18 Aérospatiale SA.321GV Super Frelons (18 was the standard complement of every IrAF squadron of the mid-1970s), Iraq is known to have received only 12, in two sub-variants. The early variant, equipped with the ORB.31 Heraclés radar, lacked floats and is illustrated here (the later version was equipped with the ORB.32 radar, some of the aerials for which were installed into floats, and will be shown in the next volume of this mini-series). All were painted in Celomer 1625 *gris bleu moyen clair* (light grey-blue) overall, with a camouflage pattern in grey-green similar to (thought lighter than) BS381C/283, and blue similar to deep saxe blue (BS381C/113) on top surfaces and sides, and large black panels around the engine exhausts. All Iraqi Super Frelons wore a double set of national markings on the fuselage sides. Fin flashes were usually applied over the variant designation and the construction number on the fin, while their known IrAF serials (always applied in black on the boom) were in the range 2020–2027. (Artwork by Tom Cooper)

The largest IRIN warships to see action during the first months of the war with Iraq were US-constructed corvettes of the PF-103-class, of which four were in service: *Bayandor* (81), *Naghdi* (82), *Milanian* (83), and *Kahnamuie* (84). Each of these 83.8m long and 10m wide vessels displaced 900 tons standard, or 1,135 tons at full load, and had a crew of 140. They were equipped with the SPS-6 search radar and SPG-34 fire-control system, and armed with two 3in (76mm) guns, and a quadruple Bofors 40mm automatic cannon. This illustration shows the IRINS *Naghdi* as of 1980, before the installation of two additional Soviet-made twin 23mm ZU-23 autocannons in place of anti-submarine mortars in 1981. The ship saw very intensive service during September and October 1980: together with *Bayandor*, she covered the evacuation of Iranian navy vessels from Khorramshahr in mid-September. On 23 September 1980, she was damaged by an Iraqi air strike while in a dry dock in Bushehr. Following quick repairs, IRINS *Naghdi* was back to sea by mid-October, and involved in escorting caravans to BIK. The ship's crest is shown inset. (Artwork by Ivan Zajac)

Perhaps the most famous of the entire Kaman-class of fast missile craft (or 'missile boats') – as the Iranians named their La Combattante II vessels, ordered in February 1974 – was IRINS *Peykan*. Laid down on the slips of Construction de Mécanique Normandie on 15 October 1974, it was launched on 12 October 1976 and commissioned into service on 31 March 1978. Vessels of this class had a standard load of 234 tons, and a full load of 255, and could reach a maximum speed of 34 knots. They were 47m (154ft) long and 7.1m (23.3ft) wide, and armed with one 76mm and one 40mm gun. Because of the revolution, only nine out of 60 BGM-84A Harpoon missiles ordered for them actually reached Iran, and *Peykan* was the second to fire one in combat: during Operation Morvarid, it sank an Iraqi P-6 motor torpedo boat. *Peykan* was subsequently sunk by Iraqi P-15 Termit anti-ship missiles, with the loss of 31 of her crew. The inset shows the crest of the 26th Missile Boat Squadron, to which IRINS *Peykan* was assigned. (Artwork by Ivan Zajac)

IRAN-IRAQ NAVAL WAR VOLUME 1: OPENING BLOWS SEPTEMBER–NOVEMBER 1980

No fewer than 140 vessels of the Projeckt 205 Tsunami-class fast missile craft ('Osa I') were constructed and, together with the following Projeckt 205ER Tsunami, they became some of most-widely exported Soviet-designed warships ever. Starting in 1974, Iraq acquired a total of six (Soviet/Russian and German sources usually list only four) and they received hull designations *R-12*, *R-13*, *R-14*, *R-15*, *R-16*, and *R-17*: these numbers were regularly overpainted or expanded through the addition of fake prefixes and a third digit, such as 'P613', for example. These 38.5m long vessels displaced 209 tons at full load, had a crew of 26, and could accelerate to a maximum speed of 42 knots. Each was equipped with four KT-97 hangars/launchers for P-15 missiles and two twin, water-cooled AK-230 30mm automatic cannons. The missiles were guided by the Rangout radar system, and the guns were directed by the MR-104 Rys fire-control system. As far as is known, the Iraqi Navy lost two of its Osa Is during the war with Iran: reportedly, both during the first months of the conflict. (Artwork by Ivan Zajac)

Between 84 and 87 Projeckt 205ER-class ('Osa II') missile boats were constructed in the USSR, and Iraq acquired eight of these, all in the 'tropicalised' sub-variant. Although their displacement was increased to 243 ton at full load, and their crew to 28, they retained the maximum speed of 42 knots. The Projeckt 205ER retained the electronics of the earlier Projeckt 205 (including the Rangout radar for missiles and Rys fire-control system for guns) but had new KT-97M launchers for P-15U missiles, and a slightly redesigned superstructure. Both versions proved popular in service and relatively easy to maintain and operate, and were able to deploy their primary armament over a range of 30 to 40km even in sea state 4 or 5. The primary weakness of both the Projeckt 205 and 205ER was the short range of their gun armament: this proved insufficient to counter even helicopters armed with guided missiles, let alone vessels of the Kaman-class which had a much heavier 76mm cannon. (Artwork by Ivan Zajac)

vii

The P-6-class – also known as Projeckt 183 Bolshevik in the USSR – was the last mass-produced wood-hulled motor torpedo boat class after the Second World War. Originally, each was armed with two tubes for 533mm torpedoes and two 2M-3 twin 25mm autocannons. Starting in 1949, over 420 were manufactured in total. They displaced 68.2 tons and could reach a speed of 43 knots. The Iraqi Navy acquired a total of six P-6s between 1959 and 1962, and was generally satisfied with them, but also happy to replace them with Projeckt 205-class missile boats, which offered much superior firepower. Indeed, all six P-6s were kept in service into 1980, even though they had their torpedo tubes removed. Relegated to the role of patrol boats, and now in far-from-ideal condition, Iraqi P-6s still saw some action during early clashes with the Iranian navy, but two were confirmed as destroyed in October and November 1980. (Artwork by Ivan Zajac)

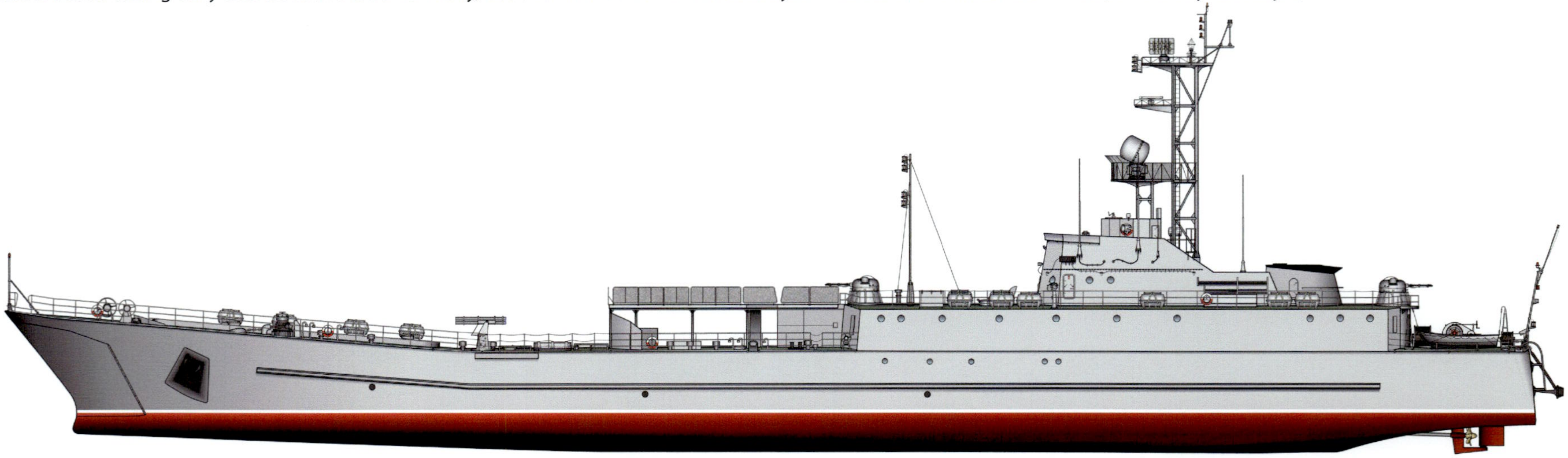

The Polnocny-class amphibious warfare vessels were designed in Poland and constructed in cooperation with the USSR between 1967 and 2002. No fewer than 107 had been built by 1986, in several variants. Iraq acquired four Polnocny-D-class ships, each of which was 81.3m long, displaced 1,233 tons at full load, and had a maximum speed of 16 knots. Contrary to earlier A-, B, and C-variants, the Polnocny-D-class had a helicopter platform, and the vessels acquired by Baghdad were armed with a single Strela 2 SAM system (ASCC/NATO codename 'SA-N-5 Grail', essentially a navalised SA-7), two AK-230 guns for air defence purposes, and two Ogon multiple rocket launchers each with 18 140mm tubes. Each could carry up to 12 armoured personnel carriers or four main battle tanks; alternatively, they could load 250 fully armed troops together with support weapons like mortars. Although slow, they were relatively spacious vessels with a good communication suite, and thus were frequently used as command ships during the war with Iran. (Artwork by Ivan Zajac)

A beautiful study of one of 20 Agusta-Sikorsky ASH-3D Sea King helicopters purchased by Iran between 1976 and 1978. As clear from its nose-mounted search radar and serial number – 8-2303 – this example belonged to the first batch and is seen wearing the service title in use since 1979. Originally equipped for ASW and SAR roles, the Sea King proved a highly versatile helicopter in Iranian service. (Tom Cooper collection)

A rare, right-hand view of an Iranian P-3F in its ultimate camouflage pattern, but still wearing pre-1976 serial 5-261. Clearly visible are two outboard underwing pylons, the large searchlight installed under the right wing, and – underneath the large black nose housing the antenna of the AN/APS-115 surface search radar – a window for the surveillance camera. (Claudio Tosselli collection)

This was the third of six British Hovercraft Corporation BH.7 hovercraft ordered by Iran in 1970 – and the first of the Mk. 5 version, originally planned to be equipped with US-made BGM-84A Harpoon anti-ship missiles. The 'Islamic' Revolution of 1979 left Iran with only a minimal stock of Harpoons, and thus these vessels primarily served in a logistic role. (Amir Kiani collection)

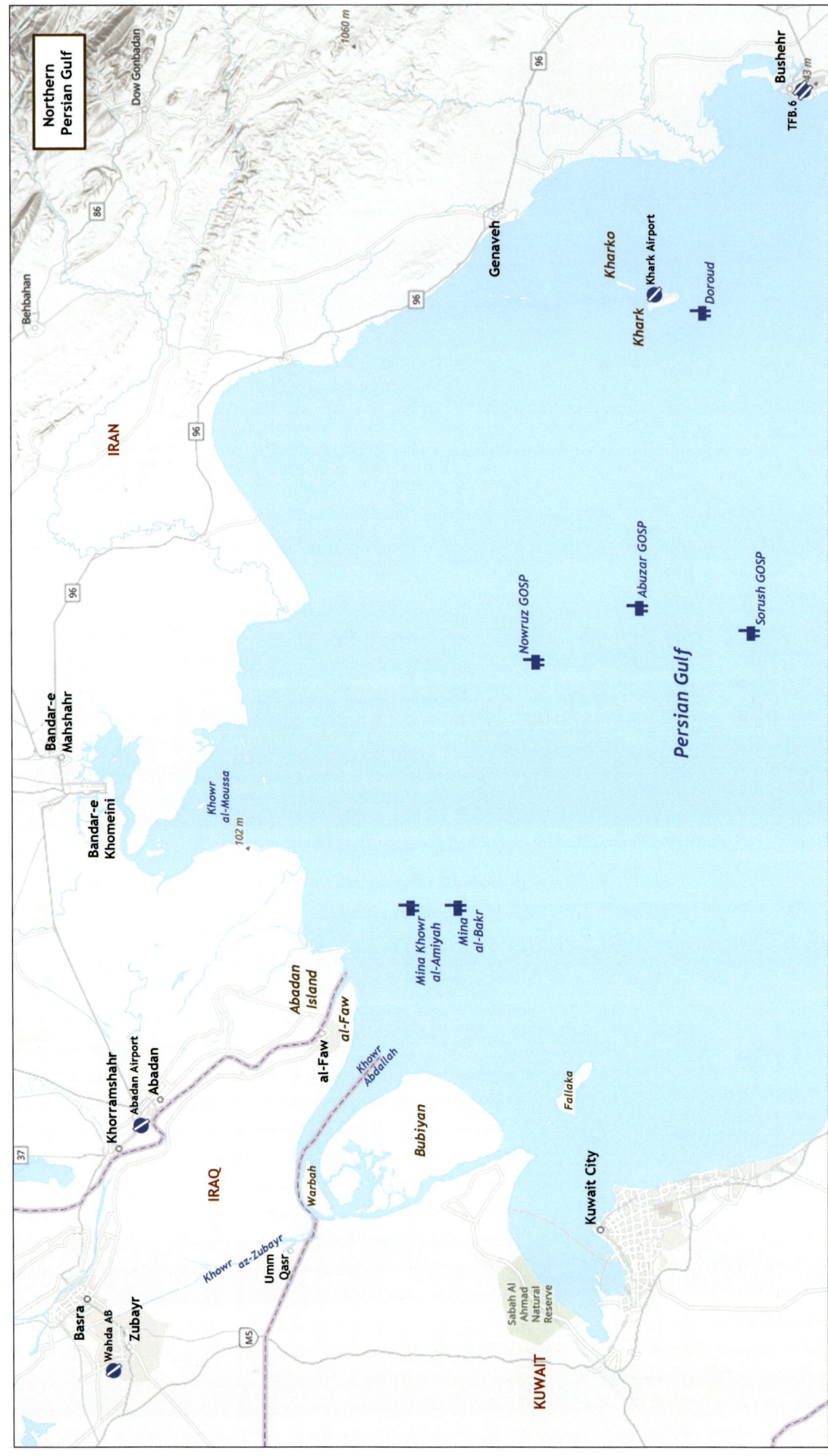

(Map by Tom Cooper)

- Directive 1: Behroz; search for and destroy enemy vessels through all of the Persian Gulf;
- Directive 2: Peykan; search for and destroy enemy vessels in the northern Persian Gulf;
- Directive 3: Ajdar; securing the movement of Iranian vessels throughout the Persian Gulf;
- Directive 4: Marjan; protecting important warships of the navy, while destroying enemy warships;
- Directive 5: Lak Lak; defence of Khark Island;
- Directive 6: Shahab; patrol activity around Khark Island for the purpose of protecting it from naval attacks.

EMERGENCY SHIPPING MOVEMENT CONTROL PLAN AND FIGHTING DIRECTIVE PEYKAN[3]

With hindsight, it could be said that for the Iranian navy the war with Iraq began as early as of 16 April 1980, when the HQ of the IRIN ordered an evacuation of all eight SR.N6 hovercraft forward deployed at the Naval Station Khosrow Abad, on the Shatt al-Arab, south of Abadan, to Khark Island. Eventually, it turned out that only two were immediately operational: they were evacuated under protection of the corvette IRINS *Bayandor*, while ground crews launched efforts to repair the other six.[4] Two days later, on 18 April 1980 – working in accordance with plans Abouzar and Zolfaghar – Captain Afzali's staff issued detailed orders for the event of a war. The first priority was to become the reorganisation of the commercial traffic along the Iranian coast. The work on this issue eventually resulted in the Emergency Shipping Movement Control Plan for the Persian Gulf (ESMCP). The ESMCP assumed that the enemy would try to, 'destroy economic and military resources of the Islamic Republic of Iran, sabotage and sink ships bound for Iranian ports'. Furthermore, it concluded that both the navy and civilian authorities lacked the experience in situations of this kind, and thus there was an overarching need to prevent any kind of major damage or loss for the country.

This aim was to be achieved through the establishment of a strictly centralised command and control authority with special purpose. Designated Task Force 421 (TF.421), the command node in question was to control all naval operations, regardless of what military branches or civilian bodies were involved. Amongst others, the order for its establishment – Fighting Directive Peykan – specified also the active use of radar stations on the *Ardeshir* and *Nowruz* offshore platforms to track and report enemy activities, and daily helicopter patrols of the area around the Iraqi Mina Khowr al-Amiyah and Mina al-Bakr offshore loading terminals. Moreover, all the vessels and coastal stations within the area of responsibility of TF.421 were to be advised to maintain constant radio communication with the HQ.

Therefore, it can be said that the IRIN expected to – right from the start of the war – impose strict control over all maritime activities and that it expected that, for the purpose of better coordination of all operations and improved security, all the relevant authorities – including the IRIAF, PMO, Islamic Revolutionary Guards Corps (IRGC), Gendarmerie, regional governmental offices, fishing industry, shipping lines and companies, and all custom offices – were to strictly follow orders of the navy. This went so far that no ships or motor launches – regardless their size or purpose – were to leave or enter any port without explicit permission of TF.421. The command and control of TF.421 was to be exercised from two control centres (see below for details), each of which was to include liaison officers from the IRIN, Gendarmerie, and IRGC. Their primary duties were:

A) preparation of standing orders and selection of suitable routes for all commercial traffic;

B) receipt and transmission of all shipping reports and weather forecasts;

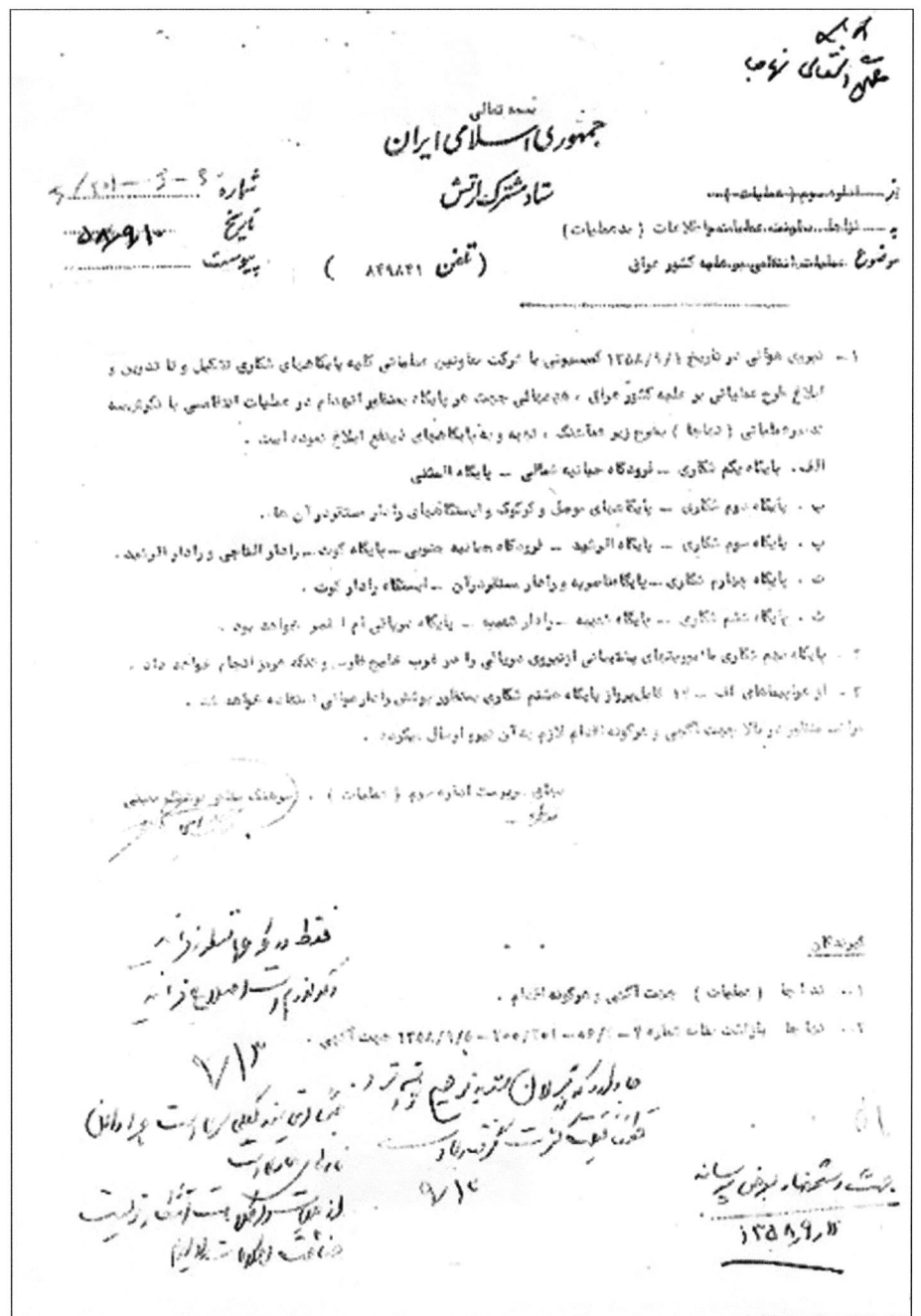

Copy of the JCS order for Plan Entegham, from 1 December 1979, detailing targets for all the active IRIAF units. (Centre of Holy Defence Documents of the Navy)

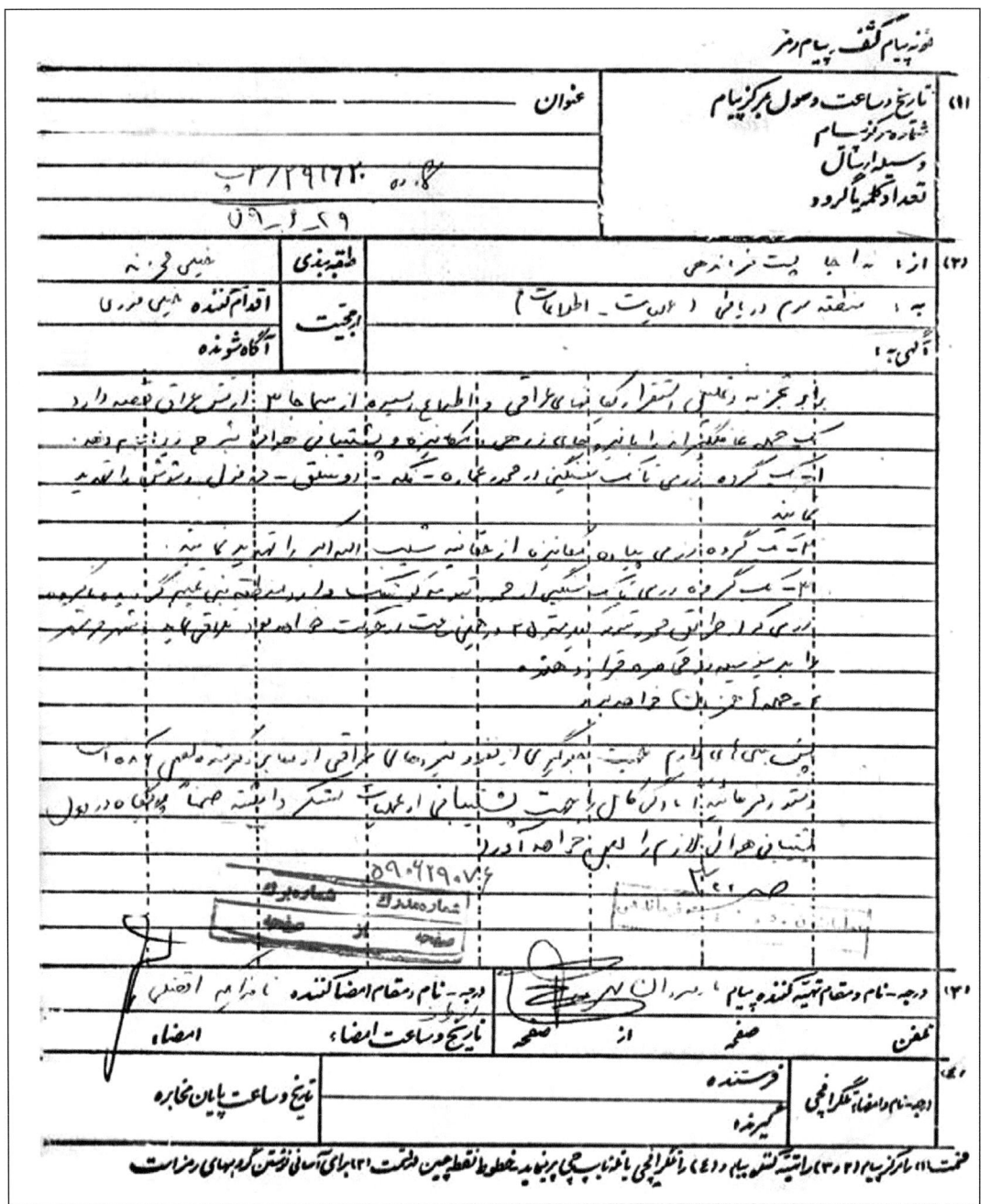

A scanned copy of Document 1, issued by the commander of the IRIN, Captain Afzali, on 18 April 1980. In this, Afzali made a clear warning to the HQ 3rd Naval District in Khorramshahr, that there was a build-up of the Iraqi Army along the border and an Iraqi attack was imminent. Furthermore, he mentioned that the TFB.3 (Hamedan) had been ordered to provide air cover, destroy enemy forces, and provide close air support on request. (Centre of Holy Defence Documents of the Navy)

C) selection of rendezvous areas for all ships expected to travel in convoys, depending on the general war situation and presence of enemy forces.

Under the ESMCP, the PMO was tasked with the following duties:

A) selection of suitable vessels for carriage of priority cargo;
B) determination of loading and unloading destination for every ship;
C) taking charge of all port duties (including loading and unloading);
D) maximisation of the usage of available vessels;
E) control of all movement of personnel and ships;
F) monitoring all the fishing zones and activity of fishery vessels (with help of the IRIN);
G) preparation of secondary facilities for loading and unloading, and for bunkering of ships, in the event of combat damage.

SADDAM'S DECISION TO INVADE

In the meantime, through early 1980, the crisis between Baghdad and Tehran continued to escalate with the two adversaries conducting terrorist operations against each other's officials. After the foreign ministers of both countries narrowly survived assassination attempts in April 1980, Iraq supposedly registered 10 violations of its airspace, and thus concluded that a 'Persian aggression was in the making'.[5]

Who exactly could have violated Iraqi airspace as of that time remains unclear: what was formerly the mighty IIAF, but now officially the IRIAF, was in tatters and out of condition to do so. Paralysed by purges of its top commanders during the revolution, subsequently the mass of its mid-ranking officers was either arrested and executed, or forced to leave the service. Moreover, the majority of air bases were occupied by various groups of armed civilians and non-commissioned officers, and it took months to re-establish a working chain of command. Amid an almost complete collapse of order and discipline, and a de-facto civil war that raged in Iran between 1979 and 1983, the IRIAF was in no condition to operate effectively even against the relatively small Kurdish uprising in north-west of the country.[6] The situation only worsened after the failed coup attempt organised by a group of about 400 officers of the air force and the army at Tactical Fighter Base 3 (TFB.3), outside Hamedan, in June 1980: this resulted in another, sweeping purge of the mid-ranks. By July 1980, the air force that used to total about 100,000 officers and other ranks was down to 30,000; all training flights stopped; all maintenance activity ceased, and the mass of the IRIAF's aircraft were stored – or left to rot wherever parked. Therefore, although it is perfectly possible that some border incidents were caused by over-zealous officers or local Iranian clergy – often out of eagerness to attract Khomeini's favour – there is little doubt about who attacked whom in September 1980.[7]

Indeed, after monitoring the wholesale collapse and disorganisation of the Iranian armed forces for a while, and concluding that the Iranians would be easy opponents, Saddam arrived at the decision to invade Iran in June 1980. The dictator in Baghdad revealed his plan to his closest aides during the meeting of the Ba'ath party leadership in Abu Ghraib on 6 July 1980. As a pretext, on 4 September 1980, Baghdad accused Tehran of shelling the vicinity of two villages which Iraq was supposed to receive from Iran in accordance with the Algiers Treaty of 1975, and which its army required as a springboard for its attack: when Tehran – preoccupied with the post-revolutionary chaos – ignored demands for their handover, the Iraqi Army, supported by Mil Mi-25 helicopter gunships of the IrAAC, seized both places three days later.[8]

TEHRAN'S FAILURE TO REACT AND BAGHDAD'S ESCALATION[9]

Having no fewer than 163 different sources within the top ranks of the Iraqi regime and its armed forces, SAVAMA quickly found out about Saddam's decision and warned all the top authorities in Tehran. When nobody reacted, the Director of the Intelligence Department of the Islamic Republic of Iran Army, Colonel Mohammad Mahdi Katibeh, addressed top members of the Majlis – the Parliament of Iran. Their reaction was anything but what might have been expected: accusing him of planning a coup against the new government, they booed him out of the building. Nevertheless, Katibeh remained persistent and eventually managed to convince Mustafa Chamran Saveei – the first Minister of Defence in the new government of Iran, and Ayatollah Khomeini's representative to the Supreme Council of National Defence – to act. On 2 September 1980, the JCS ordered the IRIN to execute Plan Zolfaghar.

As far as is known, regarding the security of the Iranian side of the Persian Gulf, nothing happened for the next two weeks, until 15 September, when the HQ of the Navy ordered the 3rd Naval District to evacuate all of its warships from the port of Khorramshahr to the sanctuary in Bushehr. Led by the corvettes *Bayandor* and *Khamanuie*, a convoy including all operational vessels left port the same afternoon, leaving behind only three light auxiliary ships (*Lavan*, *Hormuz*, and *Kish*), and six SR.N6s that were still undergoing repairs at Khosrow Abad.

Two days later, on 17 September 1980, the Iraqi radio station at the port of al-Faw began issuing warnings to all ships entering the Shatt al-Arab to sail only with an Iraqi pilot on board, and under the Iraqi flag. It remains unclear to what degree this order was respected: what is certain is that on the same day Captain Afzali issued a direct order to Captain Mostafa Madani Nejad to act according to the ESMCP and set up Task Force 421. Ironically, Nejad then took three days to assemble his staff and set up a command centre in the basement of a building in Bushehr naval base. However, once everybody was in place, thanks to the ESMCP, his staff proved capable of very quick decision-making. TF.421 was officially established on 21 September 1980 and – thanks to another timely warning by SAVAMA, which stressed that an Iraqi invasion was imminent – not only put all the warships of the IRIN on alert, but also created TF.643 for the defence of the crucial Khark Island. From that point onwards, and exactly following the definitions of the ESMCP, the TF.421 assumed responsibility for two operational areas: the northern, controlled from the Control Centre in Bushehr, stretched from BIK to Bandar-e Kangan. The southern Control Centre was established in Bandar-e Abbas, and assumed responsibility for the area between Bandar-e Kangan and Bandar-e Gwater. Command, control, and communication within the area of responsibility of TF.421 was distributed as follows:

A) Command of escort and protective forces was in the hands of the TF.421;
B) Bushehr port facilities were under the supervision of local governmental offices;
C) Bandar-e Abbas port facilities were under the supervision of the governmental office of the Hormuzgan Province;
D) Bushehr Centre (for shipping movement) was put under the control of the 2nd Naval District;
E) Bandar-e Abbas Centre (for shipping movement) was put under the control of the 1st Naval District.

At the tactical level, TF.421 assumed the following responsibilities:

A) Making sure that only small ships and motor launches were used for transferring cargo *between* Iranian ports;
B) Ascertaining that ships underway in the southern part of the Persian Gulf followed protected routes within Iranian territorial waters;
C) Securing a smooth and intensive process of imports and exports of strategic goods;
D) Securing full cooperation between the PMO and control centres for shipping movement.

Point D was considered the key for successful execution of the ESMCP.

Meanwhile, after obtaining an agreement from Khomeini, on the morning of 6 September 1980, the National Security Council authorised the President of the IRI, Abolhassan Banisadr to activate the armed forces according to Plan Abouzar. By then, it was too late: even if the top officers of the IRIAF, IRIN, and the army now knew almost everything about the Iraqi invasion (except the date on which this was to take place), except for the command structure and warships of the navy, very little was left of the army and air force (except their stored equipment), and it took days and then weeks to recall thousands of recently purged officers and other ranks. And if the severely disrupted chain of command was not already enough, the civilian authorities continued belittling or ignoring all the warnings by SAVAMA and disrupting the mobilisation of the armed forces.

Unsurprisingly, Saddam was encouraged by the apparent absence of an Iranian reaction and ordered additional probing attacks. By 10 September 1980, Iraqi troops had taken six border posts in the central sector of the mutual border, and then captured a forward communications intelligence station of the Iranian military intelligence, killing dozens of Iranians in the process. On 8 September 1980, the IRIAF was ordered into action, but in the following days lost two F-4E Phantom IIs and three F-5E Tiger II fighter-bombers to Iraqi and friendly ground fire. Even then, and despite an entire series of warnings by the 92nd Armoured Division about growing concentrations of Iraqi Army troops along the border, the government in Tehran was distrustful. Unsurprisingly, all the Iranians managed in return was for one of their F-14A Tomcat interceptors to hit an Iraqi Mi-25 with gun fire, mortally wounding its pilot, while two others shot down a single Iraqi MiG-21R and an Su-22 out of many that were now moving freely inside Iranian airspace.[10]

Table 7: Islamic Republic of Iran Navy, Order of Battle, 22 September 1980[13]		
Unit	Ships	Notes
1st Naval District; HQ Bandar-e Abbas		
?? Destroyer Squadron	*Damavand, Babr, Palang*	
?? Frigate Squadron	*Alvand, Alborz, Sabalan, Sahand*	
?? Patrol Boat Squadron	1 PBR Mk II, 6 PBR Mk III	
?? Amphibious Squadron	*Hengam, Larak*, 8 LCVP	
?? Mine-Countermeasures Squadron	*Karkas, Simorgh*	
?? Replenishment Squadron	*Bandar Abbas, Bushehr*	
9th Support Squadron	*Chabahar, Kangan, Tahei, Delvar, Sirjan, Dayer, Dilim, Charak, Chiroo, Souru*	
IRINA; NAS Bandar Abbas		
?? Helicopter Squadron	AB.212ASW	
?? Helicopter Squadron	ASH-3D	
?? Mine-Countermeasures Squadron	RH-53D	
IIAF; TFB.9 (operationally subordinated to the IRIN)		
91st ASWS	6 P-3F	
91st TFS	18 F-4E	another 18 in storage
2nd Naval District; HQ Bushehr		
1st Marine Battalion		
?? Patrol Squadron	*Khanamuie, Milian, Naghdi, Bahram, Nahid, Perwin, Keyvan, Mahan, Tiran, Mehran*	*Bayandor* in dry dock; *Mehran* from 3rd Naval District
26th Missile Boat Squadron	*Kaman, Xoubin, Khadang, Peykan, Joshan, Falakhon, Shamshir, Gorz, Gardouneh*	
?? Patrol Boat Squadron	3 PBR Mk II, 14 PBR Mk III	3 PBR Mk II and 6 PBR Mk III from 3rd Naval District
?? Mine-Countermeasures Squadron	*Harishi, Riazi*	
?? Amphibious Squadron	5 LCM, 9 LCVP	
IIAF; TFB.6		
61st TFS	F-4E	nominal 16 aircraft per squadron
62nd TFS	F-4E	but precise details on availability
63rd TFS	F-4E	unknown
3rd Naval District; HQ Khorramshahr		
2nd Marine Battalion		
8th Patrol Squadron	-	all but three vessels evacuated to Bushehr
?? Hovercraft Squadron	14 SR.N6 & BH.7	based at Khosrow Abad; evacuated to Bandar-e Khomeini

MISSING IRAQI PLANNING?

In comparison to details about IRIN war plans, next to nothing is known about what exactly the Iraqi Navy was planning to do at the start of the war. General Janabi was involved in Saddam's plotting for the opening blow. However, it seems that for security reasons, he never converted his knowledge into any kind of contingency planning or anything more detailed. Still, considering the activities of the Iraqi Navy in the first days of the conflict, and reports about the regular deployment of at least one SO-1-class patrol ship near the offshore loading terminal of Mina al-Bakr – to act as an early warning picket ship – it can be concluded that Janabi's primary concerns were possible Iranian strikes at the oil industry along the coast.[11]

Contrary to the navy, which could do little to rapidly expand or improve its position in general, during the summer of 1980 the Iraqi Air Force had significantly bolstered its assets deployed in southern Iraq. First, it deployed its No. 148 Missile Brigade – including three battalions (or 'SAM sites') equipped with Soviet-made S-75 surface-to-air missiles (ASCC/NATO codename 'SA-2 Guideline') and no fewer than five battalions equipped with S-125 (ASCC/NATO codename 'SA-3 Goa') for the defence of Basra and, especially, Wahda Air Base. Air defence of Umm Qasr naval base was bolstered through the deployment of three SA-3 SAM sites. In August 1980, after the IrAF received the first five MiG-23MF interceptors from the USSR, No. 39 Squadron – commanded by Major Ma'an Abd ar-Razzaq al-Awsi and equipped with older MiG-23MSs, which proved

Table 8: Iraqi Navy, Order of Battle, 22 September 1980		
Unit	Ships	Base & Notes
1st Naval Brigade	6 P-6	al-Faw
2nd Naval Brigade	3 SO-1	al-Faw
3rd Naval Brigade	*Ganda, Jananda*	Basra
	Atika, Nouh	Umm Qasr
	1 base defence battalion	Basra
	2 base defence battalions	Umm Qasr
	1 base defence battalion	al-Faw
4th Naval Brigade	R-12, R-13, R-14, R-15, R-16, R-17 (Osa I), R-18, R-19, R-20, R-21, R-22, R-23, R-24, R-25 (Osa II)	Umm Qasr
5th Naval Brigade	3 Zhuk	Basra
	2 Zhuk, 2 Poluchat, 2 Nyrat II	Umm Qasr
6th Naval Brigade	*Al Yarmouk, Al-Kadisia*	Umm Qasr
	3 Yevgenya	Umm Qasr
No. 101 Squadron	12 SA.321GV	Umm Qasr
77th Naval Infantry Brigade		al-Faw

a maintenance nightmare and next to useless as interceptors – was relegated to ground attack. Although homebased at Taqaddum AB, west of Baghdad, starting from 20 September 1980, this unit was distributed into several flights, one of which was forward deployed to Wahda AB.[12]

5

THE OPENING ROUND

While SAVAMA had known about Saddam's decision to invade since June, for reasons of security the mass of commanders of the Iraqi armed forces were informed about their new tasks only on 20 September 1980, when the related orders were delivered to them by courier. Following rushed preparations, they launched the invasion into south-western Iran (mainly Khuzestan province) as planned, during the afternoon of 22 September 1980 – and then in quite some confusion: the majority of the involved officers were convinced they would be commanding a 'pre-emptive' attack, designed to 'prevent a Persian aggression'. Their primary problem was that, based on an underlying assumption that this would result in a quick and easy victory, the invasion was undertaken without a clear strategic goal or aim. The IrAF did its best to follow its much belated orders for the opening air strike, and bombed about 20 Iranian air bases, radar stations, and army aviation bases, but before long realised that it lacked the aircraft, armament, training *and orders* necessary to keep even the much-weakened IRIAF under serious pressure. Similarly, the Army trundled into Khuzestan province lacking up-to-date maps – but in hope that something might turn up.[1]

Instead of turning and running away, united by the challenge of an aggressor on their soil, the Iranians put up fanatic resistance. Within a few weeks, the main prongs of the Iraqi advance were stopped due to severe casualties. Although the regular Iranian army and air force were in tatters, the air force did its best to fight back. On the contrary, the IRIN – the service the least-impacted by post-

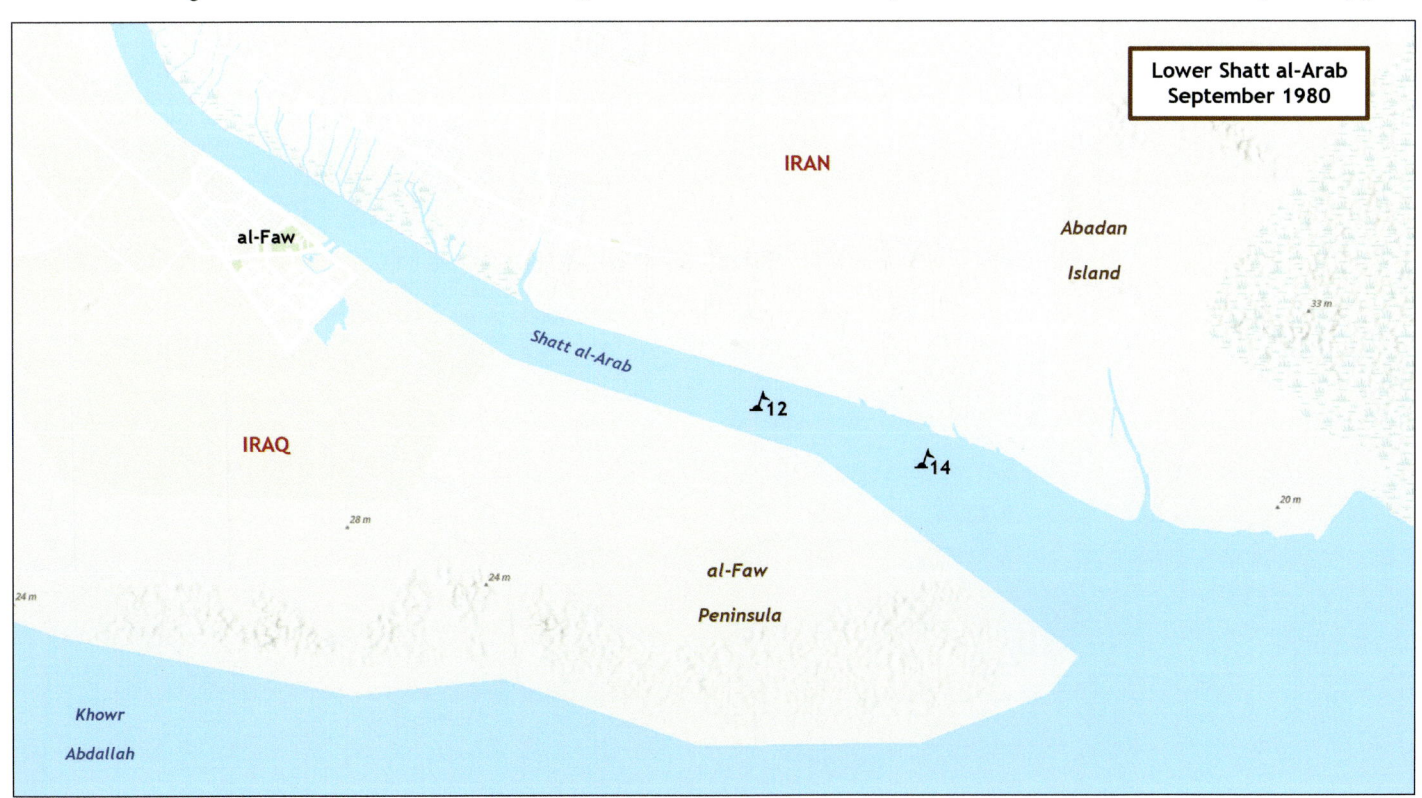

Based on an Iranian Admiralty Chart, this map shows the mouth of the Shatt al-Arab with positions of Buoys Number 12 and 14: the scene of the first clashes between the Iranian and Iraqi navies, on 20 September 1980. (Map by Tom Cooper)

revolutionary unrest – operated almost exactly as planned since it was put on alert in spring 1980. Even so, there was much inexperience and resulting confusion. On the other hand, the Iraqi armed forces found themselves facing impossible odds while operating on the basis of unclear ideas: especially the navy was almost entirely left to act on its own. Unsurprisingly, it struggled, right from the start.

IRIN'S FIRST SHOTS[2]

As mentioned above, before the revolution of 1978–79, Iran acquired about 26 US-made PBR Mk II and Mk III-class patrol boats. All were still in service as of 1980, and they were the first to see action against Iraq. On 12 September, the PBR Mk III with hull number 255 was sent up the Shatt al-Arab to investigate a border-violation in the area of the Kayyen Border Post, north of Khorramshahr: on arrival there, it was ambushed by the Iraqi Army units and had five crewmembers killed or wounded. In an even more appalling incident, on 19 September 1980, the PBR Mk III hull number 265 was ambushed near Minoo Island, and all eight of its crewmembers killed by Iraqi machine gun fire. The loss of so many sailors and a precious boat in turn became the reason for the IRIN to send a letter to Tehran, opposing the government's request to continue sending its vessels – especially bigger ones – upstream into the Shatt al-Arab.

Although no war was declared by that point in time, after the massacre of 265's crew, the gloves were off. On 20 September 1980, the HQ of TF.421 received a report that 'two Osas' of the Iraqi Navy had seized a PBR operated by the Iranian Gendarmerie

Pilots of the IRINA's sole unit equipped with AB.212ASWs, around an AS.12 ATGM installed on one of their helicopters. (IRINA Photo)

A PBR Mk II of the IRIN, underway near the mouth of the Shatt al-Arab before the war. Note the 12.7mm machine gun installed forward and a 106mm recoilless gun aft of the superstructure. (IRIN Photo)

An Agusta-Bell AB.212ASW of the IRINA (serial number 6-2403), seen firing a training version of the AS.12 ATGM. (IRINA Photo)

that ran aground near Buoy Number 14, at the mouth of the Shatt al-Arab. Therefore, the IRINA received the order to send four AB.212ASW helicopters, each armed with two AS.12 anti-tank guided missiles and supported by a pair of F-4Es from TFB.6 (Bushehr), to destroy Iraqi vessels. Eventually, only two helicopters were launched, led by Captain Askar Mohtaj; serial numbers 6-2411 and 6-2417 took off from TFB.6 at 06.00hrs local time, and flew north-west along the coast. The further they advanced, the worse the visibility became, and eventually Mohtaj and his wingman were advised to land at Naval Station Khosrow Abad and wait for the weather to improve. After a short break, they launched again at 06.50hrs, turned west and started their search for Iraqi vessels.

Eventually, Mohtaj (in 6-2411) detected the two Osas and – without any warning – ordered his co-pilot and gunner to deploy both AS.12s. Fired from a range of about 4,000 metres, at least one missile scored a hit. In turn, realising they were under attack, the Iraqis fired back but their AK-230s were much too short-ranged: one of their vessels was hit and then ran aground near Buoy Number 14 while trying to evade the second missile. However, as Mohtaj was reporting his success on the radio, he lost concentration for a moment – and collided with high power wires: the helicopter crashed, killing all three crewmembers, including the pilot, his co-pilot 1st Lieutenant Azizi, and flight technician Sergeant Gerowkani. The naval war between Iran and Iraq thus began with the IRIN losing a PBR and most of two crews, and then a precious helicopter and its crew, while rendering one of the Iraqi Navy's most important vessels non-operational: the Iraqis recovered their damaged Projeckt 205 FAC only several days later, once the area was considered safe for the necessary work, and then towed it to Umm Qasr for repairs.

FIRST STRIKE

On the afternoon of 22 September 1980, Iraq opened its invasion with a three-wave strike including either 192 or 202 combat sorties against a total of 25 targets in Iran, amongst them were TFB.1 (Mehrabad), TFB.2 (Tabriz), TFB.3 (Hamedan), TFB.4 (Dezful), TFB.6 (Bushehr), TFB.7 (Shiraz), TFB.8 (Esfahan), and TFB.11

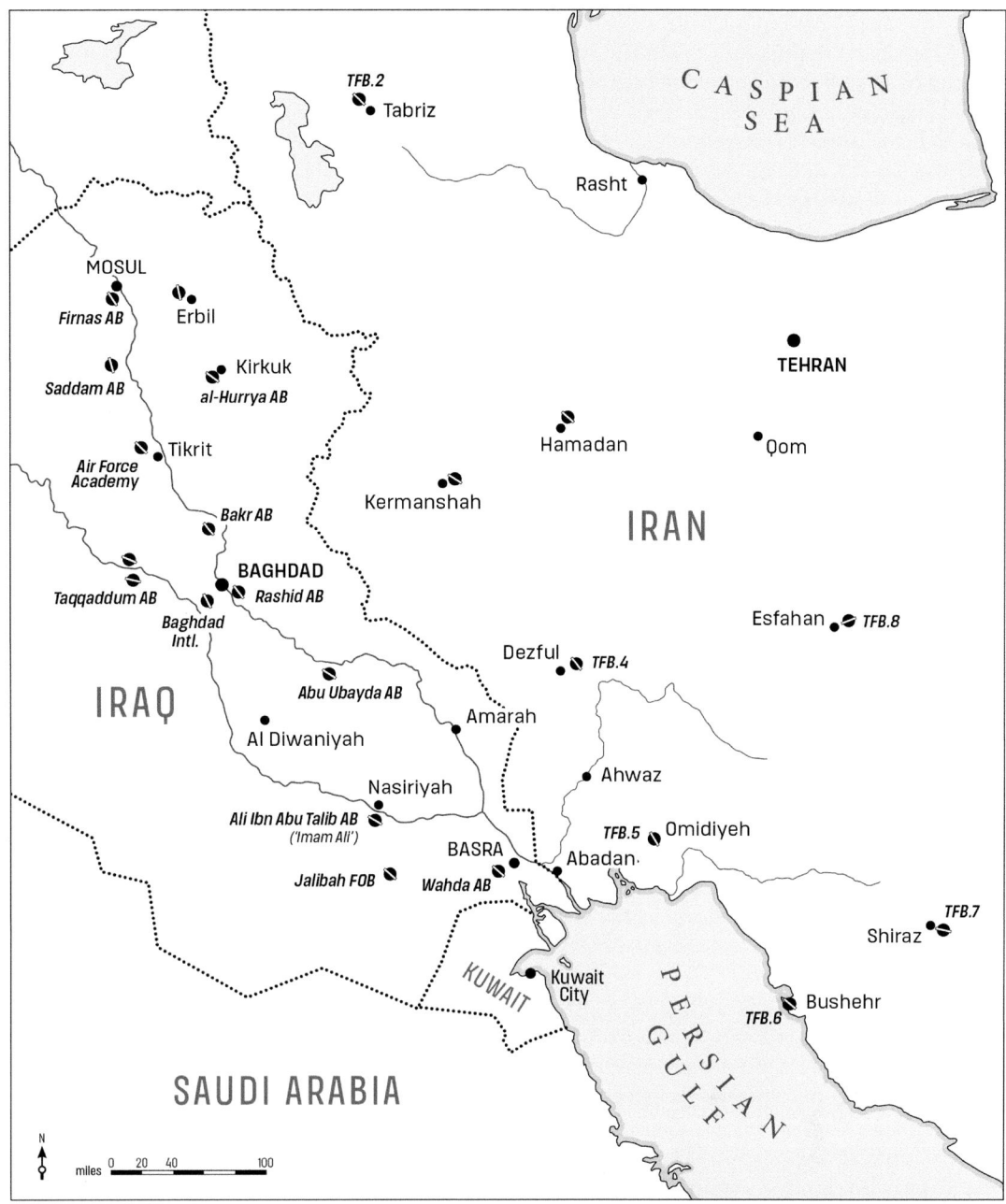

A map of major air bases in Iran and Iraq as of 1980. Notably, Bakr and Ali Ibn Abu Talib AB in Iraq were still under construction, just like TFB.5 outside Omidiyeh in Iran. The latter was never completed, and primarily used as a forward operating base by both the IRIAF and the IRIAA during the war. (Map by Micky Hewitt)

(Dowshan Tappeh, Tehran), the Islamic Republic of Iran Army Aviation (IRIAA) bases in Kermanshah and Masjed Soleyman (the 1st and 2nd Combat Support Base, respectively), several forward operating bases, the Subashi early warning radar station, the MIM-23B I-HAWK SAM site in Dehloran, and Ahwaz International Airport (IAP). Directly relevant to naval warfare were air strikes on TFB.6, TFB.7, and TFB.8, all of which either had minimal effects or even failed to reach their target. Something similar was true for the fourth such effort: the two Tupolev Tu-22 bombers tasked with the strike on TFB.9 flew via Qatar and the United Arab Emirates down the entire length of the Persian Gulf to land at Seeb Air Base in Oman. However, nobody in Baghdad thought about at least informing the Omani authorities about this operation, not to mention actually securing their agreement and support. Moreover, all the ground personnel at Seeb were British: ultimately, the latter agreed to provide only enough fuel for the two supersonic bombers to return to Iraq.

There was similar confusion in the Iraqi port facilities, which were full of merchant vessels, because although several days beforehand demanding that all foreign ships entering the waterway fly the flag of Iraq, Baghdad had not taken the precaution of emptying its ports prior to the invasion. It was only around the noon of 22 September 1980 that all the shipping on the Shatt al-Arab was suspended. Unsurprisingly, the Iraqi order caught the crews of dozens of vessels in and around the waterway, busy loading and unloading dry cargo and oil – or wanting to do so – for the limited facilities in Basra meant that many merchants had to wait for up to five months. The next – more ominous – hint of trouble came as formations of Iraqi aircraft passed by at low level heading east. A few minutes later, they were followed by the first volleys of artillery shells and unguided rockets as the Iraqi Army began the preparatory bombardment of Iranian ports before its assault. After a short break, the Iranians began replying in kind. The gloves were now off.

TRAPPED IN THE SHATT AL-ARAB

IRIN technical personnel of the Hovercraft Squadron had been trying hard since April to repair the six SR.N6s left behind at the Naval Station at Khosrow Abad. Amid the growing chaos all over the country caused by the general ignorance of the new regime towards the armed forces, the occupation of the US Embassy in Tehran followed by the failed American hostage rescue operation in April 1980, and then the Nojeh coup plot of June–July 1980, this proved a major problem. This unit's base and stocks were at Khark, but the navy had stopped all movement of its ships up the Shatt al-Arab in April, and its helicopters were much too busy to fly in any supplies of spares. Eventually, the only solution was to 'cannibalise' one of the vessels and use it as a source of spares to make another operational. The work on the first repaired SR.N6, hull number 01, was finally completed on the afternoon of 22 September: however, as soon as the hovercraft moved out of its hangar, it was shelled by Iraqi artillery and destroyed. Indeed, over the following hours, the Iraqi shelling reached such proportions that the Iranians found no other solution: they destroyed the one hovercraft that was used as a source for spares, and left the other four stored inside hangars, in the hope that they could return and repair them at some other opportunity.

Meanwhile, the outposts deployed along the northern coast of the Persian Gulf reported four Iraqi vessels approaching the PMO's pilot tender *Azadeh*, moored at the entrance to Khowr al-Mousa. The vessel was raked by 30mm gunfire, which killed its master, Captain Hamid Malekzadeh, and Chief Officer, Shaker Shahabi. Badly damaged, *Azadeh* was barely afloat when found by one of the IRIN's warships a few hours later: the Iranians towed it to BIK but all attempts at repairs eventually failed and it was scrapped.

The first Iraqi attack did not remain unanswered. Upon receiving a report about the activity of the Iraqi Navy, TFB.6 scrambled a pair of F-4E Phantoms towards the Shatt al-Arab. The crews of these claimed to have 'sunk an Osa', while the Kaman-class IRINS

Captain Malekzadeh, skipper of *Azadeh*, was one of the first Iranian seamen killed during the war with Iraq. (Centre of Holy Defence Documents of the Navy)

Azadeh's Chief Officer, Shaker Shahabi, killed in Iraqi attack on 22 September 1980. (Centre of Holy Defence Documents of the Navy)

After the loss of six SR.N6s, and because one of two examples evacuated a few days before the invasion was subsequently cannibalised as a source of spares, the hovercraft in this post-war photograph remained the sole vehicle of this class in service with the IRIN. (Photo by Ebrahim Noroozi)

Joshan claimed two others as destroyed after pursuing them into the night all the way to the mouth of Khowr az-Zubayr. Later the same evening, Tehran followed the IRINA's war-planning and announced a blockade of Iraqi ports – thus effectively declaring any merchant vessels there to be legitimate targets. Moreover, Iran announced even the waters of the lower Persian Gulf – from Abu Musa, via Sirri Island to the Cable Bank Light, to Farsi Ialand and Ras al-Kuh in the Straits of Hormuz – a maritime war zone, and demanded that all ships about to enter announce themselves 48 hours in advance. In this fashion, the Iranians aimed to protect their shipping and their ports.[3]

On the morning of 23 September, there followed an exchange of blows as the IRIAF deployed 140 combat aircraft into an aerial offensive against the air bases of the IrAF, while the IrAF reattacked some of the Iranian air bases hit the previous afternoon. Later during the day, the Iranian F-4Es bombed the port of al-Faw, while Su-22s of No. 109 Squadron attacked the port of Bushehr and damaged the corvette *Naghdi*, which was in dry dock, and the minesweeper IRINS *Shahrokh*. In turn, a Kaman-class fast missile craft then attacked merchants anchored in Iraqi territorial waters around the mouth of the Shatt al-Arab, damaging *Oriental Star* and *Lucille* with fire from 76mm guns.[4]

Early on 24 September 1980, three formations of F-4Es from TFB.6 bombed the Iraqi Navy bases and port facilities in Basra, Umm Qasr and al-Faw. Obviously distracted by the many vessels in sight, IRIAF pilots went after merchant ships instead of the much smaller Iraqi warships: the total of 72 M117 general-purpose 375lb (170kg) bombs they released hit dozens of vessels, of which 12 were sunk and 11 were badly damaged. Twenty-four hours later, four Phantoms repeated the strike, this time hitting the Kuwaiti merchant *Ibn al-Haitam* in the Shatt al-Arab. The carnage only increased once the IRIAF redirected its attention from IrAF air bases to the Iraqi petrochemical industry and tanker ships. By 18 October, almost every civilian vessel anchored in the al-Faw area – including the Iraqi tankers *Murlindhar*, *Safinat al-Umar*, *al-Phirosh*, *al-Hafifa*, *Safinat al-Nasri*, and the Indian *Gelanininpirpasa* – was hit, badly damaged, and abandoned by its crew.

FATEFUL KHORRAMSHAHR[5]

For the next few weeks, most of the public's attention was attracted to the developments in the Khorramshahr area. Together with nearby Abadan, this was the only Iranian city within 50 kilometres of the border, and then a very important one: even as of 1980, it was still the largest commercial port in the country. The port of Khorramshahr consisted of docks and long rows of storage depots constructed along the eastern bank of the Shatt a-Arab, some also extending along the northern bank of the River Karoun. A single bridge spanned the Karoun to the southern part of the city and nearby Abadan: indeed, to Abadan Island, which stretched for over

A view from the port of Khorramshahr over the Shatt al-Arab to the Iraqi side. (Photo by Sirous Ebrahimi)

An aerial view of ships, jetties and storage depots in the port of Khorramshahr, seen before the war. (PMO)

One of four crews of IRINA AB.212ASW helicopters deployed to support the 92nd Armoured Division in action against the Iraqi onslaught north of Khorramshahr, together with their helicopter and one of the AS.12 ATGMs, in late September 1980. Notable atop of the cabin are the sight used to guide missiles (quadratic grey box), and the dome of the SMA/APS surface search radar (black housing). (IRINA Photo)

A rare photograph from the port of Khorramshahr early during the Iraqi invasion, showing one of the warehouses set on fire by Iraqi shelling. (PMO)

behind only medical and security personnel. The local garrison comprised the 165th Mechanised Battalion of the 92nd Armoured Division (with about a squadron of Chieftain main battle tanks), 260 cadets of the Officers' School, and a company of 185 gendarmes, equipped with a few 106mm recoilless rifles and infantry weapons. They were reinforced by about 300 – later up to 3,000 – civilian volunteers, the majority of whom had no military training, were ill-equipped, and operated in uncoordinated groups. At least as important were reinforcements that began entering Khorramshahr from early October: these included 175 personnel from the IRINA's base in Khosrow Abad, who withdrew there after abandoning the Naval Station of Khosrow Abad. Eventually, the garrison was reinforced by a 700-strong battalion of the Iranian 1st Marine Brigade from Bandar-e Abbas, and a company of SBS. However, the commanding officer of the Iranian Marines in the city, Commander Hooshang Samadi, experienced immense problems while trying to cooperate with the civilian volunteers – at least until the militias were consolidated under the command of Mohammad Jahanara and 25 Pasdaran – members of a para-military organisation formalised as the IRGC, on 1 January 1981 – who established their headquarters in the Grand Mosque, in the city centre. Eventually, Jahanara proved authoritative enough to assume the command over all the Iranian forces in Khorramshahr.

70km on a north-west to south-east axis, in between the Shatt al-Arab in the west and the Bahmanshir River in the east.

Predominantly populated by a wealthy, cosmopolitan class, Khorramshahr experienced numerous incidents – mainly bombing attacks – before the invasion. By 17 September 1980, when Saddam Hussein demonstratively declared the 1975 Algiers Treaty to null and void on Iraqi National TV, the frequency of Iraqi attacks reached a point where the authorities ordered an evacuation of the population: this was completed by around 25 September, leaving

The city and the port were not only important because of their proximity to Iraq: Khorramshahr was a major connection between Abadan and Ahwaz, with a well-developed road and railway infrastructure (even if no major pipeline). That said, it was smaller than either of the other two cities, it contained no important military facilities, even if local warehouses – reportedly – contained large stocks of spare parts for the IRIAF, unloaded at the time of the revolutionary unrest in late 1978 and early 1979, and not collected since. However, this was a prestigious and symbolic target, and it offered the best prospects of capturing Abadan, the primary Iraqi aim in this part of Khuzestan. In turn, for the Iranians, it was important as a symbol of resistance to the invasion, as much as to tie down and exhaust the invaders.

THE CITY OF BLOOD

Following a substantial artillery preparation, the reinforced Iraqi 3rd Armoured Division advanced into the empty area north of Khorramshahr in the face of weak Iranian resistance, as the army withdrew towards areas easier to defend, including hills further north and east, and Khorramshahr in the south. Obviously, this was an operation related to ground warfare, nevertheless, the Iranian navy became involved. First, four of its AB.212ASWs were assigned to support the 92nd Armoured Division. The reason was that all the Bell AH-1J Cobra attack helicopters assigned to the 2nd Combat Support Base of the IRIAA, in Masjed Suleiman (halfway between Dezful and Ahwaz) were found to have a malfunction of their M65 sight, and thus were non-operational. Unless they could be brought to the helicopter factories in Esfahan for repairs and brought back to operational service, it was down to the AS.12-armed helicopters of the navy to help the few army units trying to stem the Iraqi onslaught in the direction of Ahwaz and around Khorramshahr. The crews did their best, flying dozens of reconnaissance and observation sorties, and nine direct attacks. In total, they fired 12 AS.12s, to hit six Iraqi tanks and one ammunition truck. Meanwhile, RH-53Ds were brought in from Bandar-e Abbas to haul army personnel to reinforce elements of the 92nd Armoured in Darkhovin, Bostan and Mahrshar. In at least one case, their quick action saved an entire tank battalion from being surrounded by the advancing Iraqis.

Such efforts were too little though: on 25 September 1980, the Iraqis reached the Karoun River, east/south-east of Khorramshahr. Inside the city, the Iranian troops were meanwhile busy erecting barricades, digging trenches, and constructing sangars for tanks and mortars. Advancing methodically, the Iraqi Army approached the outskirts only on 28 September, but subsequently began pounding the city and the port with M-46 130mm guns, 160mm mortars, and BM-21 multiple rocket launchers. While this left Khorramshahr shrouded in fire and smoke, it caused no damage to any of the ships blockaded inside the port. That changed during the first major Iraqi assault, launched during the night from 29 to 30 September by commandos that attempted to cross the Shatt: the resulting battle caused a fire that wrecked *Capriolo*, causing the crew to evacuate to the nearby *Steel Trade*, while *Iran Badr* was run aground and abandoned, as was the *Taha*.

Following another vicious artillery barrage, the Iraqis assaulted again on 1 October. Over the following two days, they managed to secure the railway station, most of the port along the Shatt al-Arab, and the local radio station. However, as far as is known, nobody in Baghdad or Basra had the idea of helping to evacuate any of the foreign merchants stranded in the port. With this the obvious became a matter of fact: more than 90 merchantmen (see Appendix 1) were trapped inside the Shatt al-Arab, of which about 70 were on the Iranian side, foremost in Khorramshahr. All but one were unable to escape because of repeated air strikes, and almost constant risk of artillery, mortar, or rocket fire, and because navigating the narrow waterway full of silt that could block it, required expert pilots who refused to board the ships.[6]

On the contrary, over the next 10 days, Khorramshahr and ships in its port came not only under sustained Iraqi air and artillery attacks, but also several Iranian barrages: by 14 October, at least 18 vessels were badly damaged and abandoned. Over the following three days, Iraqi commandos managed to destroy most of the Iranian Chieftains, cause heavy losses to civilian volunteers, and

Wreckage of the Iranian merchant *Iran Ghayam*, seen still sitting on the bottom at the port of Khorramshahr in 2019. (Photo by Sirous Ebrahimi)

Laying nearby is another Iranian merchant, *Iran Hejat*, sunk during the siege of September–October 1980. (Photo by Sirous Ebrahimi)

The wreckage of merchants in the Shatt al-Arab, against the backdrop of Khorramshahr's ruins, seen after the liberation of the city, in 1982. (IRIN Photo)

The IRIN was largely successful in evacuating its fleet from the naval base in Khorramshahr in April 1980. However, some older vessels were in no condition to move. Thus, the light auxiliary ships *Lavan* (401) and *Hormuz* (402) – the wrecks of both of which are shown in this photograph taken after the liberation of Khorramshahr in 1982 – were scuttled in order to prevent them from falling into Iraqi hands. (Tom Cooper collection)

secure the main highway into the city centre, earning it the nickname 'City of Blood' in Iran. By 21 October, they began assaulting the Government Building and the bridge spanning the Karoun River, despite heavy losses mainly caused by Iranian volunteers who excelled in ambushing and sniping the enemy. The bridge was secured by the dawn of 24 October: until that point in time, the IRIN was still able to bring in reinforcements, ammunition and water to the defenders of Khorramshahr (apparently, stocks of food were sufficient for an even longer siege) with the help of BH.7 hovercraft that were moving at high speed up and down the Bahmanshir River: both of its banks were densely populated and full of vegetation and thus provided plentiful cover. However, the loss of the bridge left the exhausted defenders isolated. Short on ammunition, they began evacuating over the Karoun to the southern side of Khorramshahr. The battle ended by the morning of 10 November, after 34 days of bitter fighting, several thousands of casualties, the complete ruin of the most important Iranian commercial port of the time, and the loss of about 70 Iranian and foreign merchant ships in its port.

TURTLES THAT SAVED ABADAN[7]

Following evacuation of all the operational hovercraft from Khosrow Abad to Bandar-e Khomeini, starting from 15 April 1980, hovercraft of the sole IRIN squadron equipped with them were first busy with the evacuation of civilians from Khark Island, before – starting from 22 September 1980 – helping deploy the 1st Marine Battalion from Bushehr to BIK, and to Khorramshahr. Underway by night, frequently in bad weather, next they began evacuating civilians from Abadan. This operation

A pre-revolution photograph of the Iranian Navy's BH.7 hovercraft with hull number 104. These big and loud but very fast vessels were to prove their worth during the sieges of Khorramshahr and Abadan. (Tom Cooper collection)

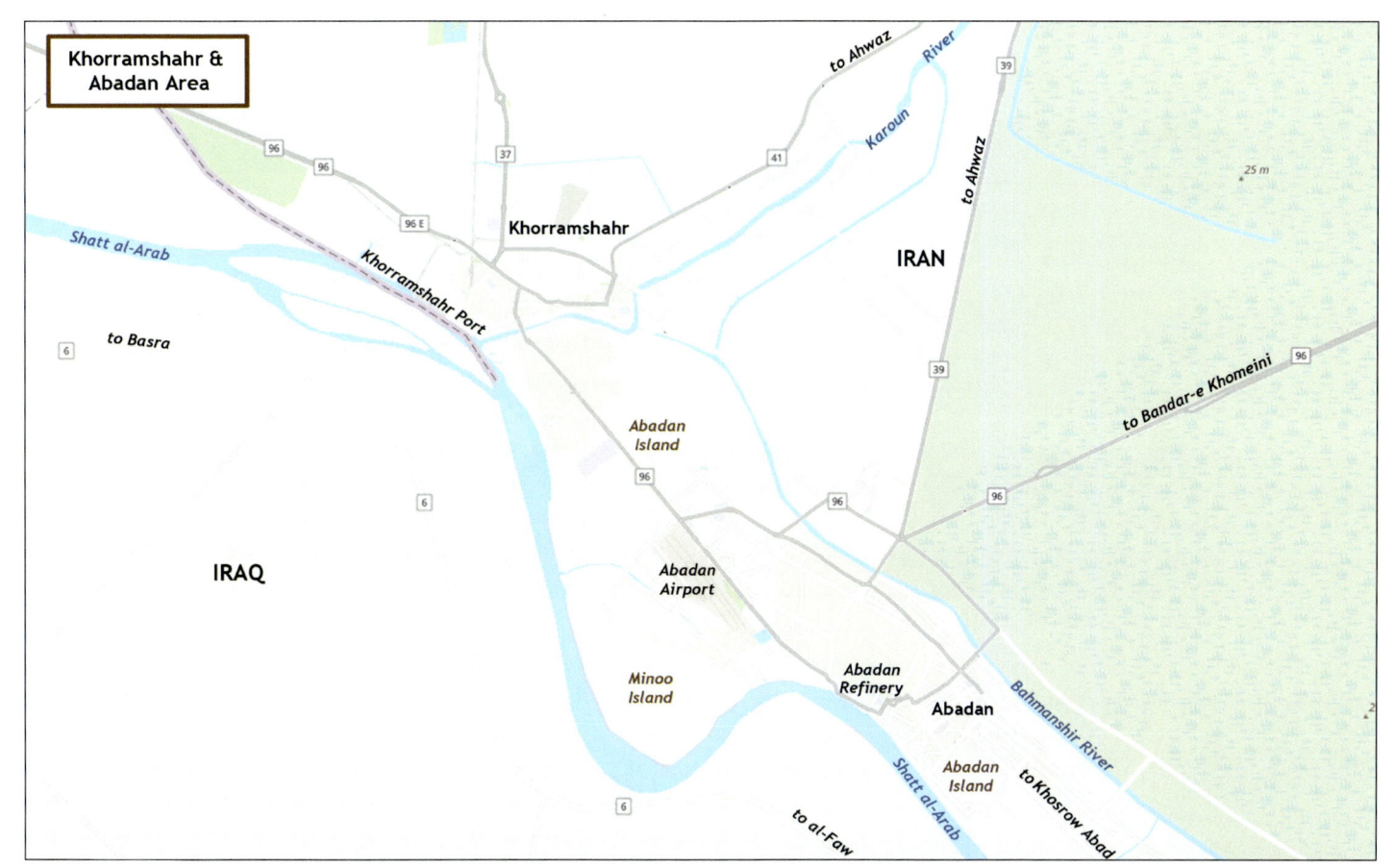

A map of Khorramshahr and Abadan, with the northern tip of Abadan Island, Abadan Airport, and the confluence of the Karoun and Bahmanshir rivers. The crews of IRIN hovercraft made extensive use of the latter both during their efforts to keep the defenders of Khorramshahr resupplied, and during the evacuation of civilians from Abadan. (Map by Tom Cooper)

was further intensified once the Iraqis managed to cut off the road connecting this city with Bandar-e Mahshahr in mid-October 1980, and then crossed the Bahmanshir River at the Istgah-e Haft Bridge, south of Abadan, and brought the road to Khosrow Abad under their fire in mid-November. From that point onwards, the only IRIN vessels capable of reaching the besieged Abadan were hovercraft – which quickly earned themselves the nickname 'turtles' (both for their symbolic strength and after the migratory sea turtles laying eggs on the shores of Farsi Island). The usual supply run from Bandar-e Khomeini up the Bahmanshir River to the small port of Choibedeh was undertaken by night, regardless the weather, and usually took six hours. For two weeks of the second half of November 1980, each

Arrival of Iranian Army troops and Marines to Abadan, by hovercraft from Bushehr, on 21 September 1980. (Centre of Holy Defence Documents of the Navy)

Evacuation of civilians from Abadan, in October-november 1980. (Centre of Holy Defence Documents of the Navy)

of the five available hovercraft performed two sorties per night, for an average total of 10, until enough helicopters and barges became available to take over. On the way back, they were evacuating civilians, the wounded, the bodies of those killed, and prisoners of war. Ultimately, the hovercraft squadron flew 900 hours in support of the garrison of Abadan, nearly all of them under Iraqi fire, yet without a single loss. The efforts of their crews proved crucial in the defence of the city, and their services were highly appreciated even by the civilian authorities.

6
ORGANISING CARAVANS

Perhaps the most unusual aspect of the Iran-Iraq War – and certainly its most under-researched facete – is the fact that for the entire duration of the conflict the Islamic Republic of Iran Navy conducted a major convoy operation between the ports of Bushehr and Bandar-e Khomeini. This is even more so considering that this effort was crucial for Iran's capability to continue waging the war, and that it resulted in some of the fiercest air-to-air, air-to-sea, and naval battles of this conflict, as well as most of the attacks against international merchant vessels. However, and while details of one or another related air combat might have become known over time, this context remains essentially unknown outside the relatively small communities of the IRIAF, IRIN and veterans of the Iranian commercial and merchant services: it is certainly unrecognised by the mass of foreign monitors and naval services. While much of the related statistics remain unknown, what has become available by now makes the scope of what the IRIN termed Operation Crocodile plainly clear: by mid-July 1988, it resulted in the safe delivery of over 300 million tons of cargo to Iran, and up to 10.4 million tons of cargo, by a total of 692 vessels, to BIK.

OPERATION CROCODILE[1]

Initial planning for Operation Crocodile was undertaken in May 1980, almost immediately after the ESMCP was adopted, and finalised in the form of Directive Azhdar. It envisaged the organisation of maritime traffic between the ports of Bushehr and Bandar-e Khomeini in the form of convoys (colloquially 'caravans' in Iran) escorted by navy warships, with the following aims:

1) Keeping sea lines open for commercial traffic
2) Prevention of disruption in the import/export process

While the ESMCP thus provided a solid basis for further planning, it covered only parts of the IRIN's responsibilities. The crucial issue was that of organising and securing maritime traffic to and from all Iranian ports in the Persian Gulf, but especially those inside the combat zone in the north. In this regard, the navy depended both on its own forces and the PMO. Correspondingly, Captain Afzali's staff took care to clearly define the duties of the latter, as follows:

A) Coordination of movement and communication procedures
B) Organisation of maritime operations following orders from TF.421 (this included nocturnal dredging operations, strict light control from sunset until dawn, and relevant command centres)
C) Use of jetties at the naval base in Bandar-e Abbas for berthing commercial ships, loading and unloading operations as necessary (in order to speed up commercial operations)
D) Coordination with TF.421 in regards of selection of suitable jetties in BIK, and protection of all ships during the process of unloading and their withdrawal from the port
E) Protection of fuel storage vessels, and securing refuelling of all IRIN ships as necessary

For the purpose of conducting Operation Caravan, a separate war room was set up in Bushehr, in which liaison officers from all branches of the armed forces were involved. The merchants used were any kind of commercial vessels carrying all sorts of cargos from all over the world: on average, every ship was loaded with about 15,000 tons. TF.421 and the PMO were responsible for guiding all of them first to the Bandar-e Abbas anchorage, and then to the Bushehr anchorage. With the help of the privately owned Pilotage Company in the latter port, a committee was set up with responsibility to assign ships – or turn them down – to the convoys, depending on their technical condition, experience and reliability of their crew, the nature of their cargo, availability of specific IRIN warships, and availability of pilots.

A new caravan was set up as soon as the number of ships anchored off Bushehr grew to between 15 and 20. The size of caravans then varied greatly, but – and although there are oral reports about some including 10 or more vessels – at least officially, none ever exceeded eight ships. Once at the Bushehr anchorage, every ship was assigned its own number: this helped pilots and escorting warships quickly identify them. As soon as a merchant was selected for the next convoy, it was ordered to another position on the anchorage, assigned a single, Soviet-made ZU-23 twin-barrel 23mm autocannon with ammunition and its IRIN crew. Early on, there was a shortage of such weapons and teams, and only ships carrying prioritised cargo received them. Later on, enough guns became available to be assigned literally to every single civilian ship involved. Moreover, with time, each ship embarked an IRIN team equipped with SA-7 MANPADs. Top cover was always provided by F-4E Phantom fighter-bombers from TFB.6.

As soon as the next caravan was formed – usually during the evening hours – the ships were ordered to start moving, in a line formation, with a separation of one mile between them. A convoy from Bushehr would always start its movement at the same time a convoy with empty ships would depart from BIK. The inboard route to BIK was named the Route Green, or Leg 1. Initially during the passage, the crews were not kept on alert: however, everybody was called to stations as soon as the caravan approached about 30nm (56km) south of the entrance to Khowr al-Moussa, roughly halfway between that point and Khark Island. The aim was for the inbound convoy to always enter the high-risk area – Route Red – during daylight hours. At that point in time:

- a pair of F-4Es from TFB.6 would establish a combat air patrol (CAP) north-east of the convoy's route, to provide protection against enemy air strikes
- two ASH-3D helicopters would fly a surface combat patrol (SURCAP) ahead of the convoy
- one FAC would take a position near the *Nowruz* offshore oil rig

At the entrance to the Khowr al-Moussa channel, the protection of every merchant was reinforced through embarkation of a team of marines armed with additional SA-7s and heavy machine guns, while the IRIAF usually added another pair of F-4Es to bolster top cover. Escorting warships had strict orders to protect every merchant vessel right up to the berths in BIK: only once that part of the task was completed would they turn around and prepare to escort an outbound convoy of – usually empty – ships back to Bushehr.

Notable is that none of the caravans included any kind of tanker ships: vessels hauling fuels and lubricants to BIK were always escorted to BIK by IRIN warships in separate operations. Unlike the merchants, all of them received SA-7 teams from the start until the end of the war, and received particularly strong protection, including extra top cover from the IRIAF. Moreover, regardless if they were moving from Bushehr to BIK, or back, any empty spaces in their tanks had to be filled with inert gas, as a fire-suppression measure.

THE FIRST CONVOY AND THE FIRST NAVAL BATTLE

Prior to the voyage of the first caravan, TF.421 dispatched several FACs on a reconnaissance of the route to BIK. This prompted Baghdad to claim having repelled an attempt by Iranian warships to mine Khowr Abdallah and to have sunk 'two enemy frigates'. Actually, on 24 September 1980, no IRIN vessels ventured this far north: instead, that afternoon Kaman-class FACs of TF.421 shelled the terminals of Mina al-Bakr and Mina Khowr al-Amiyah, and claimed an Iraqi 'MiG' as shot down.

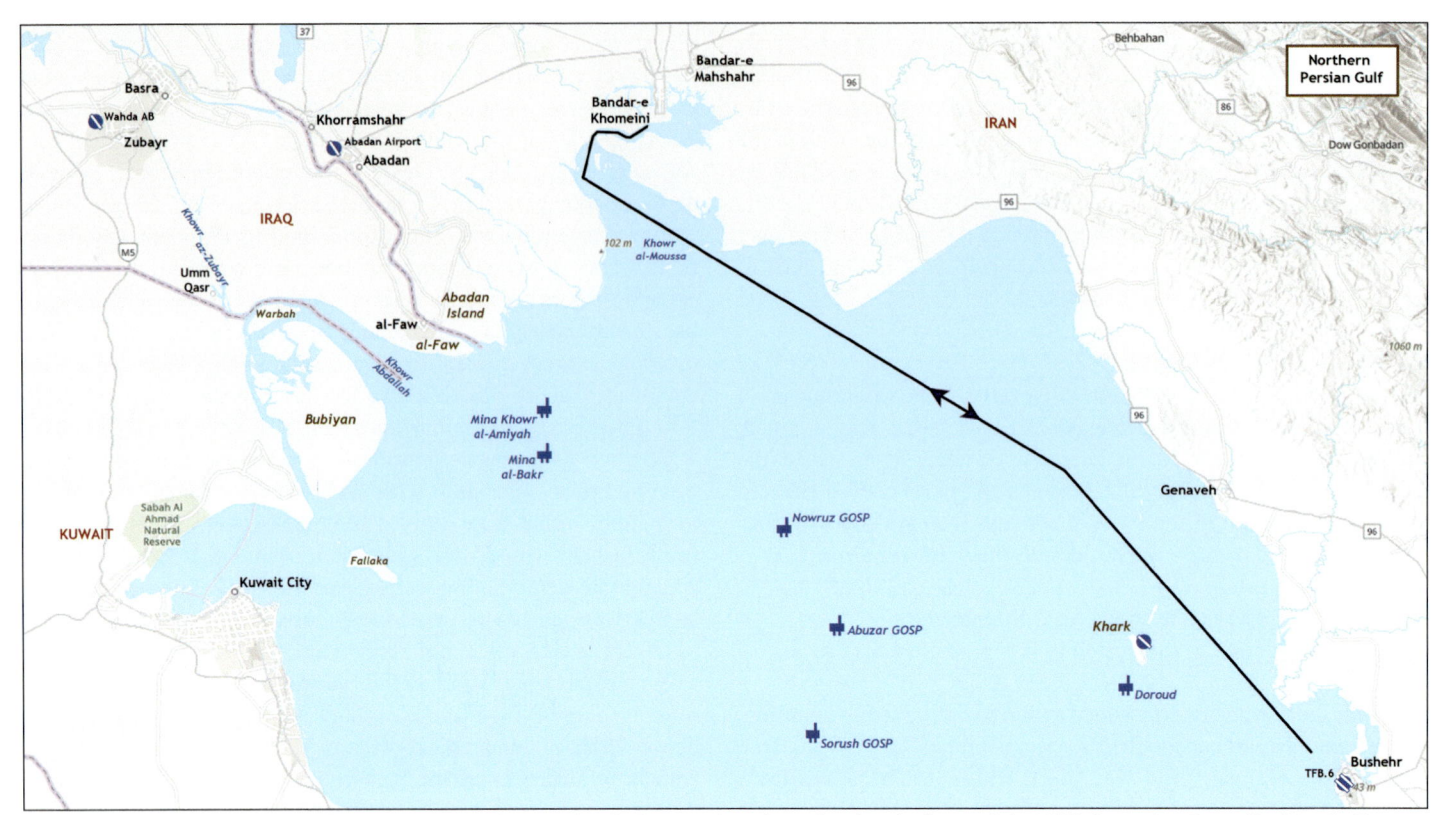

A map of the northern Persian Gulf, showing the usual route taken by 'caravans' conducted within the frame of the IRIN's Operation Crocodile. (Map by Tom Cooper)

Led by Captain Shahab Dashtestani, a highly experienced naval pilot, the first caravan moved out of the Bushehr anchorage shortly after midnight of 24 September 1980, thus starting Operation Crocodille which was to last for eight years. Sometime during the following day, on 25 September, the approach of this convoy to the Khowr al-Moussa Channel resulted in the first major clash between the Iranian and Iraqi navies. Details about this high-speed battle remain scarce, but it seems that it was fought at relatively short range and that thanks to their 76mm guns – which easily outranged the 30mm AK-630s of the Iraqi Osas, and 25mm 2M-3s on the P-6s – the Iranians proved clearly superior. Baghdad claimed the sinking of six Iranian vessels, but admitted losing a minesweeper and two P-6 patrol boats. Actually, the IRIN suffered no losses while delivering the convoy safely to BIK.

FIRST CONVOY BATTLE

Indeed, encouraged by their 'success', on 25 and 26 September the Iraqis launched a series of air strikes and naval attacks on the first caravan returning eight merchants in ballast to Bushehr. Sadly, precise details about both the Iranian and the Iraqi operations remain unclear, but available reports from the IRIN indicate sustained strikes by 'MiGs' – probably Su-22s of No. 109 Squadron, homebased at Wahda AB – and 'Osas', several of which ranged all the way south to the Khark Island area. Although the Iranians managed to avoid all the missiles and bombs released in their direction, the duration of these attacks was such that, gradually, the IRIN lost control, and its skippers lost situational awareness. To make the confusion even greater, communications with the HQ of TF.421 repeatedly failed, causing a breakdown in coordination: the ultimate result was that the crews of the warships underway in the northern Persian Gulf began opening fire at any kind of aircraft passing by.

Not informed about this chaos, the IRIAF continued its offensive on the Iraqi petrochemical industry and around 12.20hrs of 26 September, two F-4Es from TFB.6 bombed KAAOT and ABOT. Five minutes later, as the two jets were underway back to base, they passed by the Kaman-class IRINS *Keyvan*, underway near the southern approaches to Khowr al-Moussa. All of a sudden, the SA-7 team protecting the vessel opened fire: the unsuspecting Phantom crews did not react, and the leader of the pair was shot down. Major Massoud Mohammadi and his back-seater, 2nd Lieutenant Azizollah Jaffari, were killed.

Once the air was clear, around 15.25hrs, the crew of *Keyvan* proudly reported downing 'an Iraqi MiG' to HQ TF.421 in Bushehr and announced it was conducting a search operation for its pilot. This was still going on when, around 16.10hrs the IRIAF High Command in Tehran requested the navy to launch a search and rescue (SAR) operation for the crew of a missing F-4E. The SAR operation went on until the next morning, but 'only' resulted in *Keyvan* and the minesweeper IRINS *Simorgh* – the commanding ship of this caravan operation – eventually finding the wreckage of an Iranian Phantom, and bodies of its crew.[2]

The action went on, and at 08.00hrs on the morning of 27 September 1980, two F-4Es from TFB.6 bombed Mina Khowr al-Amiyah and Mina al-Bakr again. On the way back, both jets came under fire from IRIN units: the wingman was shot down by an SA-7 fired by *Keyvan*, and its crew – including – 1st Lieutenant Hassan Kadkhodaei and 2nd Lieutenant Ali-Reza Molla ali Akbari – was killed. The other jet was then felled by a Sea Cat SAM fired from the naval base in Mahshahr: this time, the crew – including Captain Ali Akbar Bashiri and 2nd Lieutenant Reza Karami – managed to eject but both the pilot and his radar intercept officer (RIO) were injured. Uncertain about what was going on, but missing two of its F-4Es, the IRIAF High Command in Tehran was left without choice: at 11.00hrs, it advised the JCS about the loss and requested that TF.421 mount a SAR operation. In the middle of this, about an hour later, *Keyvan* and *Simorgh* reported the finding of Phantom wreckage and the bodies of its crew, mentioned above. Rather unsurprisingly, this only increased the confusion….[3]

The IINS/IRINS *Keyvan*, seen before 1976, with her old hull number 61. Notable is the 40mm Bofors automatic cannon aft of the superstructure. (Leon Manoucherians collection)

Uncertain about the reason for all the losses of TFB.6, the JCS launched an investigation involving high-ranking officers from the IRIAF and the IRIN. The team travelled to Mahshahr and BIK to interview all the available participants, eventually filing a 23-page report, determining the circumstances of all three losses as follows:

1) IRINS *Keyvan* was responsible for the downing of two Phantoms. The ship was underway near the entrance to Khowr Moussa…it misidentified Phantoms for MiGs and opened fire.
2) Because there was no unified command centre for operations in the BIK area, and because most of the command nodes were preoccupied with the fierce battles further north for Abadan and Khorramshahr, air defence units and ships in the northern Persian Gulf were not properly informed about IRIAF operations.
3) There was a latent problem in the communication systems of all the involved branches of the armed forces, but especially within the IRIN: the crew of *Keyvan* was never informed about the activity of friendly fighter jets.
4) At the time the three Phantoms were shot down, all the air defence units and all the warships in the BIK area were on red alert, and rules of engagement 'weapons free' were in effect; therefore, everybody opened fire at any kind of approaching aircraft. However, at that time, the personnel had not received even a bare minimum of training in aircraft identification.
5) There was a need to declare a 'no-fly zone' for Iranian aircraft in the area of the petrochemical complex in BIK, but especially over the huge tank farm (capacity 15,000 tons) and the liquified gas tanks, so that any aircraft flying there would be considered enemy and destroyed.[4]

As a consequence of this loss, henceforth, the commanding ship of any IRIN operation in the northern Persian Gulf was assigned an IRIAF officer fully qualified as a forward air controller, and he was responsible for coordination between air and naval units.

PLAN BEHROZ[5]

On 27 September 1980, the JCS in Tehran ordered TF.421 to join the general offensive against the Iraqi petrochemical industry, and knock out the loading terminals in the port of al-Faw. For this purpose, the IRIN organised a task force including five Kaman-class FACs and two companies of marines. Late during the night of 28 to 29 September, the vessels took the Iraqis by surprise through sailing directly into the port and landing the marines there. While the troops demolished some of the facilities, the positions of Iraqi artillery and other petrochemical installations were destroyed by fire from 76mm guns at short range. The assault party was then successfully evacuated and all ships returned safely to Bushehr.

Encouraged by this success, on 30 September 1980, the command staff of the IRIN fell back upon the pre-war Plan Behroz, which included orders for all of its warships:

- Use all means at their disposal to search for and destroy whatever Iraqi aircraft and warships they can detect (and to report about this to the Task Force 421)
- Stop and seize any merchants bound for Iraq, or any Iraq-flagged ship; in the case of resistance, such vessels should be destroyed

Amongst other points, Plan Behroz stipulated aggressive operations by the IRIN, in close cooperation with the IRINA and IRIAF. For example, the skippers of Iranian warships were strictly advised:

- whenever ordered by TF.421, and in cooperation with helicopters, pursue and destroy any enemy surface or airborne combatants they can find
- while their helicopters were on patrol, to remain near offshore oil rigs, at full alert, and ready to move out immediately

For Iranian warships, detection, tracking and destruction of Iraqi Osas was assigned the highest priority: any kind of sighting of these was to be promptly reported and prosecuted by ASH-3D helicopters, which were to track the movement of enemy FACs with use of their radars and then guide other units in to attack. Finally, the skippers of all IRIN warships were ordered to request air support via HQ TF.421, as and when necessary.

Obviously, this was an overambitious plan: already busy organising and protecting merchant traffic up and down the Iranian coast, there were too few ships and helicopters to actively search for Iraqi or Iraq-bound vessels elsewhere around the Persian Gulf. However, Plan Behroz clearly indicated that the command of the IRIN expected its skippers to maintain the initiative, act aggressively, and search for and destroy Iraqi warships and other vessels at every opportunity. It had it good sides, too, for example in the form of emphasising close cooperation with the IRIAF.

CHASING OSAS
In early October, SAVAMA reported that several Iraqi Osas and merchants had taken refuge in Kuwait. Therefore, the IRIN sent a team of its own intelligence service – consisting of officers fluent in Arabic – by speedboat to Kuwait, to investigate. On its arrival in Kuwait City, the team was surprised to find itself turned down by the staff of the local Iranian embassy, who was annoyed to have them there, and refused to provide any help. Nevertheless, the officers went on and eventually returned to Iran to report that one Osa was moored at the Shaibeh oil terminal, and another in the port of Showaikah – both at least as of 5 October 1980.[6]

On 10 October 1980, an ASH-3D carrying out the now usual patrol of the area around Mina Khowr al-Amiyah and Mina al-Bakr, detected a merchant ship anchored nearby. The HQ of TF.421 ordered the Kaman-class IRINS *Peykan* to investigate. As the crew of the unknown vessel – variously reported as 'Greek' or 'Chinese' – saw the Iranian missile boat approaching, it raised anchor and tried to escape towards Khowr Abdallah. However, *Peykan* was faster: upon entering the range of its 76mm main gun it opened fire, scoring several hits. Minutes later, the unknown vessel stopped, lowered life-boats and was abandoned by the crew.

THE LOSS OF *MEHRAN* AND *TIRAN*[7]
One major issue marring not only the IRIAF and the IRIN, but also the operations by naval pilots early during the war was that everybody developed a strange urge to rush to 'complete the mission and return to base at the earliest possible moment', regardless of the risk. As a result of this, the Iraqis managed to exact revenge on 14 October 1980. Around 19.00hrs local time, the PMO-owned tugboat *Payam* sailed from BIK towing two 800-ton barges for Bandar-e Abbas. The acting operations commander of the area at the time, Captain Shahrokhi Far, skipper of the minesweeper IRINS *Karkas*, warned the *Payam* not to move on its own, but this was ignored. About an hour later, the PMO-owned pilot tender *Navid* followed in fashion, also ignoring warnings. Minutes later, both vessels were hit – each by one P-15. Five crewmembers of *Navid* were killed on the spot, including Captain Yadollah Gholizadeh. The burned-out wreckage

An ASH-3D made for Iran (serial number 8-2306), seen prior to delivery. Deployed at NAS Bushehr, the sole IRINA unit operating them flew regular surface combat patrols (SURCAPs) over the northern Persian Gulf, keeping a watchful eye on the activity of the Iraqi Navy, throughout the entire duration of the conflict. (Amir Kiani collection)

The RF-4E was a version of the F-4E Phantom II, equipped with – amongst others – a set of highly-sophisticated reconnaissance cameras installed in its nose: windows for two of these are visible under the forward fuselage of this example, photographed on take-off. Iran acquired a total of 12 RF-4Es in the early 1970s, and 10 of these were still operational with the 11th Tactical Reconnaissance Squadron as of September 1980. Up to six of these were regularly forward deployed at TFB.6. (Tom Cooper collection)

A reconnaissance photograph taken by an Iranian RF-4E during its mission over Umm Qasr on 26 September 1980. Clearly visible are (from top to bottom), two P-6-class torpedo boats (with the one at top centre still having its torpedo tubes installed); an SO-1-class patrol ship; a Poluchat-class patrol boat, two Projekt-205ER (Osa II) missile boats; and (lower right corner) three barges. (Tom Cooper collection)

disaster when the Cape-class patrol vessel IRINS *Mehran* – commanded by 1st Lieutenant Hamid Reza Eftekari – was hit by a P-15 missile and set on fire during withdrawal from the Shatt towards Khowr al-Mousa. The sister ship IRINS *Tiran* – commanded by 1st Lieutenant Faramarz Barimani (and, reportedly, renamed *Azadi* by that time) – was sent to investigate: it found the *Mehran* burning fiercely and in the process of sinking. Only four out of 15 of her crew were still alive: they and the bodies of the killed crewmembers were evacuated and *Tiran* set a course for BIK.

Intending to provide top cover for the evacuation, TF.421 requested that TFB.6 send one of its F-4Es; a Phantom II armed with four AGM-65As and two AIM-7E Sparrows was scrambled from Bushehr. Tragically, the appearance of the lonesome Iranian fighter-bomber only worsened the situation: already in shock from the horrific experience of having to evacuate badly burned crewmembers of *Mehran*, the crew of *Tiran* was nervous, and thus opened fire at the jet with their 40mm AAA. The pilot of the Phantom called the HQ of TFB.6 to report that he could see the burning hulk of *Mehran*, and a 'gunboat escaping from the area while shooting at him'. What kind of order he received in return is unclear: what is certain is that TFB.6 was not in contact with *Tiran*, while the HQ of TF.421 subsequently reported that it lost radio contact with the ship. Apparently convinced that *Tiran* was an Iraqi vessel, the crew of the F-4E then decided to attack:

floated for the next two days, until scuttled by the IRIN, which is why the official date of the *Navid*'s sinking in Iranian records is given as 16 October 1980 – which was also the date on which the tugboat *Pooneh*, underway to Bandar-e Imam Hassan, found a barge about 25 miles north-west of Khark, with 20 people on board: these were survivors of both *Payam* and *Navid*.

In attempt to suppress the Iraqi pressure upon BIK, the IRIN retaliated with another raid: at dawn on 18 October, its FACs shelled and sank five tankers in the southern Shatt al-Arab: *al-Hafifa*, *al-Nasari*, *al-Phirosh*, the *Murlindhar*, and *Sufina al-Umar*, as well as the Indian *Gelaninipirpasa*. However, this mission ended in a

A pair of F-4Es from TFB.6, armed with AGM-65A Maverick guided missiles (on inboard underwing pylons), shortly before commencing take-off. (Tom Cooper collection)

Tiran, seen in the early 1970s, still with her original hull number (62). In 1976, this number was changed to 202. Notable is the 40mm Bofors gun, installed on the rear deck. (Leon Manoucherians collection)

Captain Yadollah Gholizadeh, killed when the Iraqis hit his pilot tender *Navid* in Khowr al-Mousa on 14 October, together with five other crewmembers: Chief Engineer Gholamreza Sartagh, Chief Officer Hamzeh Ali Khah, 2nd Officer Hamid Tarfi Khasteh, and Engineer Younes Alipoor. (Sirious Ebrahimi collection)

Captain Sarnevesht, *Mehran's* skipper and the sole survivor of the blue-on-blue tragedy that befell the IRIAF and the IRIN on 18 October 1980. (Centre of Holy Defence Documents of the Navy)

after making a 270-degree turn, it acquired the vessel and fired one AGM-65A. The Maverick slammed into the bridge, instantly killing almost the entire crew. The sole survivor was Captain Sarnevesht, *Mehran's* skipper, who was picked from the water by a search and rescue helicopter later in the afternoon. Alarmed by reports about damage and losses, *Joshan* returned to the scene. Its crew could do little more than extinguish the fire on what was left of *Tiran*: the hulk was then taken under tow by a tug, and – escorted by the corvette IRINS *Naghdi* – brought to Khark Island. Eventually, *Tiran* was completely rebuilt and recommissioned to the IRIN in April 1983, as *Azadi*.[8]

FIRST HARPOONS[9]

During the first two weeks of the war, the Iraqi Navy deployed at least a dozen of its Soviet-made P-15 anti-ship missiles in combat. The results were meagre, because – as described above – although two Iranian support vessels were sunk by them, not one IRIN warship was even damaged. In turn, the Iranian navy did not fire any of nine BGM-84 Harpoons acquired from the USA for equipping its Kaman-class FACs: all the naval battles its warships fought in late September and early October saw them deploying exclusively their 76mm, 40mm, 35mm, and 23mm automatic cannons. The principal reason for this was that most of the clashes took place along the northern coast of the Persian Gulf, where the local marshes could easily distract the seeker heads of active radar homing missiles. Moreover, the majority were fought at relatively short ranges, or at least the Iranians were well-skilled in avoiding Iraqi SS-N-2 Styx anti-ship missiles, and approaching to within the range of their artillery, while avoiding entering the range of the 30mm cannons of Iraqi FACs. Finally, it seems the Iranians considered these weapons too precious and, in expectation of the war remaining short, and lack of experience in operating them, decided to conserve them. However, as the war went on into its fourth week, and with no end in sight, there was an incentive to suppress the Iraqi Navy to the degree where it could not endanger the caravans heading for BIK. The best way to do so was through the destruction of its Osa FACs. This is how the idea was born to outfit one of the FACs with Harpoons, then draw some of the Osas out to the open seas and ambush them.

The plan was set in motion during the night of 22 to 23 October: equipped with at least two BGM-84s – always packed in their transport canisters, which also served as launchers – IRINS *Joshan* moved into a position about 50nm (93km) south-west of BIK, attempting to draw Iraqi Osas out of their refuge in Khowr az-Zubayr and to the open sea. The Iraqis swallowed the bait but reacted in an unusual fashion: two of their boats moved south, but in a tight formation and a very slow speed, less than 10 knots (19km/h). *Joshan* continued drawing the Iraqis further out to sea, until they made a mistake and increased their speed. Captain Ali Akbar Akhgar wasted no time: he turned his ship around and targeted the nearest enemy vessel with one Harpoon. The missile functioned as advertised and scored a direct hit, causing one of the Osas to erupt in fire and smoke: the other promptly turned away and distanced towards the north.

Joshan remained on station for several hours longer, attempting to attract yet more Iraqi attention. Around 12.25hrs, a lonesome P-6 patrol boat ventured out of the Khowr az-Zubayr before turning around as soon as it detected an approaching F-4E from TFB.6. Piloted by Major Ali-Reza Yassini, the Phantom pressed home its attack, only to discover an Osa near the Iraqi patrol boat: quickly switching his attention to the new target, he claimed it as destroyed by a single AGM-65A Maverick missile.

7
THE IRAQI MEDUSA

Despite repeated air strikes by the IRIAF through September and October, the two oil-loading terminals south-east of al-Faw – Mina Khowr al-Amiyah and Mina al-Bakr – remained a major obstacle to the safe conduct of Operation Caravan and other IRIN enterprises in the northern Persian Gulf. These huge steel structures were about 6nm (11km) apart, with KAAOT only 10km from the southern tip of Abadan Island and less than 25km from the Iranian mainland. This terminal was 3,142ft (961m) long and 343ft (105m) at its widest point, rising 38ft (10m) above the water level during ebbtide and 20ft (6m) during high tide. It had four berths capable of loading tankers with capacity of up to 500,000dwt. ABOT had two loading platforms, each with two berths capable of accommodating tankers up to 350,000dwt. It was 975.4m long and 106.7m at its widest point. The two terminals made of thick steel pipes were surrounded by sea 105ft (32m) deep during ebbtide, and 100ft (30m) during high tide.

Thanks to two underwater pipelines connecting them to Ras al-Bisha on the Faw Peninsula, and from there to Basra, Mina Khowr al-Amiyah and Mina al-Bakr were capable of pumping up to 178,000 barrels of oil per hour. Before the war, they were responsible for two thirds of Iraqi oil exports. Obviously, the outbreak of war stopped any kind of commercial activities, but they remained valuable and were permanently garrisoned by a company of Iraqi naval infantry, and protected by several twin 23mm ZU-23 and 57mm S-60 AAA guns, and teams equipped with SA-7 MANPADs. The Iraqis installed a French-made TRS.3004 Sea Tiger E/F-band surveillance radar on one of them. While it remains unknown if the latter was truly capable of detecting ships all the way to the Bushehr anchorage, as claimed by the Iraqis, it is certain that it enabled them to detect the movement of the Iranian traffic approaching Khowr al-Mousa from the south, or exiting it; perhaps even moving within that channel. In addition to the local defences, the IrAF constantly held a pair of Su-22s on alert at Shoibiyah AB.[1]

OPERATION ASHKAN[2]

After studying KAAOT and ABOT for a while Captain Afzali's staff drew several important conclusions, including:

- 1) Damaging these two terminals would knock out the mass of Iraqi oil-exporting capability
- 2) The IRIN had to evaluate the Iraqi garrison on them, in order to find out the strengths and weaknesses of their defences, and determine their reaction times
- 3) The IRIN had to find a way to instil fear into the Iraqi garrison and, if possible, force them to evacuate the two terminals entirely
- 4) Because of the two terminals, the Iraqi Navy was able to continue operating in the northern Persian Gulf, despite the Iranian naval blockade of its ports: therefore, foreign shipping companies were refusing to send their ships into this area

The conclusion was that there was a need to destroy the two offshore terminals, or at least render them useless to the Iraqis and prevent Osas from using the massive structures to conceal themselves and then launch P-15s from there. Correspondingly, TF.42 set up a task force consisting of three Kaman-class FACs – IRINS *Peykan*, IRINS *Joshan*, and IRINS *Gardoneh* – ASH-3D helicopters from IRINA, and F-4Es from TFB.6. All the involved commanders were intensively briefed, especially on the local charts and known enemy positions.

In order to improve security of the following operation, on 31 October 1980, the three IRIN warships left Bushehr naval base one by one, instead of simultaneously as usual: *Joshan*, which acted as the command ship for this operation, at

Mina Khowr al-Amiyah, seen following its complete reconstruction by the US armed forces in 2007. (US DoD)

16.45hrs, *Peykan* at 17.00hrs, and *Gardoneh* at 17.24hrs. *Gardoneh* experienced an early engine problem and was forced to return at 17.45hrs: following hasty repairs, it was back to sea at 22.35hrs, and headed for the *Ardeshir* offshore oil platform, where a single ASH-3D and *Peykan* were already waiting for the operation to start. Once there, *Gardoneh* continued for *Nowruz*, where it joined the waiting *Joshan*.

In complete radio silence and with all their radars turned off, the three ships then began moving from one oil rig to the other, in attempt to attract Iraqi attention, but also to confuse the enemy about their intentions. *Peykan* moved first, moving to the *Sorush* oil rig before reaching *Ardeshir* around 23.30hrs; *Gardoneh* sailed to *Nowruz*, joining the *Joshan* there. Around 03.00hrs in the morning of 1 November, *Peykan* activated its Mk.92 fire-control system to make several sweeps of the area due north, but detected no targets: therefore, all three ships accelerated to full speed, and started their attack.

Joshan's target was Mina Khowr al-Amiyah; *Gardoneh* went for Mina al-Bakr, while *Peykan* – which carried several SA-7 teams and was responsible for air defence – followed them. Despite the bad weather – including sea state 4 – and darkness, the ASH-3D then passed by to assume the role of the forward air controller. The Iraqis reacted only after 06.00hrs in the morning, when the alert was sounded at Wahda AB and a pair of Su-22s scrambled to investigate. One of them detected the Iranian warships and attacked, forcing them into high-speed manoeuvring and deployment of chaff. Eventually, *Peykan*'s SA-7 operators reacted with several missiles. Reportedly, one of these scored a direct hit, smashing one of the big Sukhois into the sea before it was able to release its bombs upon *Joshan*. The crew of the ASH-3D confirmed the downing of a 'MiG' and reported that there was no ejection, but no corresponding IrAF loss is known. The next problem was the weather: this worsened over the next 30 minutes, making precise aiming of the artillery nearly impossible. Therefore, the ships waited at about five miles off their targets until 07.00hrs. When the weather did improve, they commenced the firing action, which lasted until 07.50hrs and caused numerous fires on both Iraqi terminals. Satisfied with the results, the Iranians withdrew without further incident.

OPERATION MORVARID[3]

The IRIN concluded Operation Ashkan to have been successful in disabling both Mina Khowr al-Amiyah and Mina al-Bakr, but also realised that a much more comprehensive effort would be necessary to prevent the Iraqis from making military use of the two constructions. Therefore, Captain Afzali decided to stage a

ASH-3D serial number 8-2308 seen on a landing spot at Mina al-Bakr early on the morning of 29 November 1980. (IRINA)

much more ambitious raid and assumed direct command over its planning. The result was Operation Morvarid, which was a complex enterprise, including:

- electronic warfare support by one of two EC-130H Khoofash aircraft of the IRIAF
- comprehensive barrier combat air patrols (BARCAPs) by a total of seven F-14As from TFB.7 (Shiraz) and 12 from TFB.8 (Esfahan) on the first day (28 November); and another 18 on the second day, with the task of blocking the approach of the IrAF to the combat zone
- a nocturnal insertion of special forces by IRINA's ASH-3D helicopters
- a demolition of installations with the use of reinforcements and explosives brought in from Khark Island
- an exfiltration of all the involved forces under the cover of seven F-4Es from TFB.6, and 19 F-14As from TFB.7 and TFB.8, and warships of the IRIN

The Iranians attacked at around 24.00hrs on 28 November 1980, when the lonesome Khoofash of the IRIAF suddenly jammed all the Iraqi radio communications between al-Faw, Basra and Umm Qasr. Minutes later, two AB.212ASWs (serial numbers 6-2409 and 6-2410) and one ASH-3D Sea King (serial number 8-2308, callsign Zireh-8), dashed through the darkness at critically low altitudes above the sea surface towards their targets: the two smaller helicopters deployed the Iranian SBS operators at Mina Khowr al-Amiyah, followed, seconds later, by the Sea King that landed at Mina al-Bakr. Taking the defenders by surprise, the Iranian special forces quickly brought both terminals under their control. With the

A crewmember of Zireh-8 in front of his helicopter, seen immediately after Mina al-Bakr was secured by Iranian SBS commandos. (IRINA)

Mina al-Bakr on fire, as it was left by the Iranians after their nocturnal raid of 28–29 November 1980. (IRIN)

Shatt al-Arab with – as it was to turn out – insufficient support: although ready for action, two PF-103-class corvettes and two other FACs were held back at Bushehr; only the IRINS *Zobin* was deployed to a position about 15nm (28km) west of Khark Island.

IRAQI COUNTERATTACK[4]

The sudden and massive Iranian onslaught caught the Iraqis completely by surprise. The commander of the navy, General Janubi, was woken at his home in Basra around midnight of 28 to 29 November, and quickly briefed on the situation. By then, it was clear only that contact with both Mina Khowr al-Amiyah and Mina al-Bakr had been lost. Except for this, the only thing certain was that Iraqi surveillance radars were tracking two Iranian warships off the mouth of the Shatt al-Arab. For Janubi, this was the only – but also a perfect – opportunity for retaliation. He ordered an immediate recall of all the available crews and the quick deployment of all ships. Shortly before dawn, a Polnocny-class amphibious warfare vessel, escorted by P-6 patrol boats *P-121* and *P-125*, by Osas *R-14*, *R-15*, *R-20*, and *R-21*, and two tugs, left Umm Qasr heading south. They were supported by a total of nine helicopters. One of the latter – an Aérospatiale SE.316B Alouette III – was the first to establish contact with the Iranians: it shadowed the two FACs as they were withdrawing towards the two terminals at high speed. Osas

installations in Iranian hands, three IRIN hovercraft – escorted by IRINS *Joshan* and IRINS *Peykan* (callsign Sassan) – departed Khark Island carrying reinforcements and engineers with explosives. As soon as the demolition charges were in place, the landing parties – together with a few dozens of Iraqi prisoners of war – were evacuated to the hovercraft and returned straight to Bushehr: behind them, explosives were set off, demolishing selected segments of both Mina Khowr al-Amiyah and Mina al-Bakr.

At this point in time, Operation Morvarid had progressed flawlessly. The problems began when, in expectation of an Iraqi counterattack, *Joshan* and *Peykan* were sent towards the mouth of the

were immediately rushed into a pursuit and launched multiple P-15s – all of which were thwarted by a mixture of evasive manoeuvres and chaff.

Both Iranian Kaman-class fast missile craft were meanwhile near Mina al-Bakr: close to its massive construction they were relatively safe because whatever additional P-15s the Iraqis fired at them all locked onto the metal structure of the terminal instead. In turn, they had a clear field of fire, as demonstrated when *Peykan* quickly pulled away and fired one BGM-84 Harpoon, sinking an Iraqi P-6 (the survivors of the crew were lucky for their vessel went down relatively close to the coast, and they were able to swim to safety). However, no

The Iraqi Projeckt 205-class (Osa I) missile boat *R-13* (hull designation 'P613' was applied to confuse observers), seen before the war. As far as is known, sister-ships *R-14* and *R-15* were involved in the Iraqi counterstrike launched in response to Operation Morvarid. The Iraqis confirmed the loss of one of them. (Ali Altobchi collection)

The Iraqi Projeckt 205ER-class (Osa II) missile boat *R-19*, seen before the war. Two vessels of this type – *R-20* and *R-21* – were involved in the counterattack of early 29 November 1980: both were claimed as sunk by the Iranians, but Iraqi sources denied any such losses. (Ali Altobchi collection)

matter how imprecise, repeated attacks by Iraqi missiles effectively pinned down the Iranians: by mid-morning, after several hours of this cat-and-mouse game, the skippers of the two IRIN warships requested permission to withdraw. Both *Joshan* and *Peykan* were running critically short of ammunition and chaff, and the latter was meanwhile listing at the stern due to a near-miss by a P-15 which exploded above and behind the ship, injuring several crewmembers.

BATTLE OF KHOWR ABDALLAH[5]

Colonel Fakouri – who was not only the commander of the IRIAF, but also the Minister of Defence of the Islamic Republic of Iran, and thus vastly superior in rank to Captain Afzali – denied the permission to withdraw: two Phantoms from TFB.6 (callsigns Zireh-1 and Zireh-2) were airborne and approaching, and he wanted the two warships to act as scouts for their air strikes. For unknown reasons, only one F-4E – serial number 3-6636 – then actually attacked the Iraqis. Its pilot, Captain Hossein Khalatbari, recalled:

> I was ordered to take-off for al-Bakr and al-Amiya. As I approached the area, *Peykan*'s skipper yelled on the radio, "Heading 210 degrees, range 12 miles! Four Iraqi fast missile craft! Destroy them!" I headed in that direction and identified three Osas and

one P-6 sailing in a defensive formation. Several Iraqi helicopters were nearby, but they kept their distance. As I dived on one of the Osas, it fired a missile at *Peykan*, so I warned them on the radio. My first two Mavericks both scored direct hits, and quickly sank one of the Iraqi vessels. I fired two other Mavericks at two different ships, then turned back to TFB.6. Next, I called Captain Sajedi to come and finish the last remaining Iraqi warship.

Captain Sajedi's F-4E was also armed with four AGM-65s, and the pilot claimed the destruction of not only one Osa, but also three other Iraqi vessels at the mouth of Khowr Abdullah. The Iraqis are not known to have lost any vessels in these first two attacks by Phantoms, but this might be little surprising considering that at the time TFB.6 had only two RIOs experienced in deploying AGM-65As, and others were trained by their pilots while flying actual combat sorties that morning. Moreover, the deployment of this early version Maverick against ships was both severely constrained by the missile's seeker head that required high-contrast targets that could be easily disturbed by sun reflections; and by its narrow field of view, which reduced its effective engagement range to less than 5,000 metres. Finally, it is perfectly possible that the attack by the two F-4Es was disrupted by the appearance of Iraqi interceptors, even if these are not explicitly mentioned in the IRIN report.

That IrAF fighter-bombers were active is confirmed by the IRIAF documentation, according to which its interceptors found themselves busy right after the first out of four F-4Es armed with AIM-7E-2 Sparrow medium-range and AIM-9J Sidewinder short-range air-to-air missiles, and the first F-14As armed with AIM-54A Phoenix long-range air-to-air missiles reached their BARCAP stations west of Bandar-e Khomeini. At 07.05hrs, Captain Ali-Reza Sirous (with RIO Captain Mohammad Masbogh in the rear cockpit) fired two AIM-54As to claim two MiG-23s as shot down. Around 07.22hrs, another Tomcat from TFB.7, piloted by Captain Yadollah Khalili (with 2nd Lieutenant Behroz Pashpoor in the back seat), claimed another 'MiG' as shot down as it was about to attack IRINS *Peykan*.[6]

As air battles were raging in the skies above, several missile boats of the Iraqi Navy accelerated in the southern direction to attack again. Around 08.00hrs at least three Osa fast missile craft concentrated their attacks upon *Peykan*, against which they fired a total of six P-15s. The first two overflew the Iranian warship and exploded harmlessly on crashing into the sea. The third detonated closer to *Peykan*, killing one crewmember. However, the fourth hit the FAC, causing an instant loss of steering and communication. The last two hit the bridge, completely demolishing the superstructure in the process, killing many and throwing other crewmembers overboard. Dead in the water, the burning hulk began to sink. It was

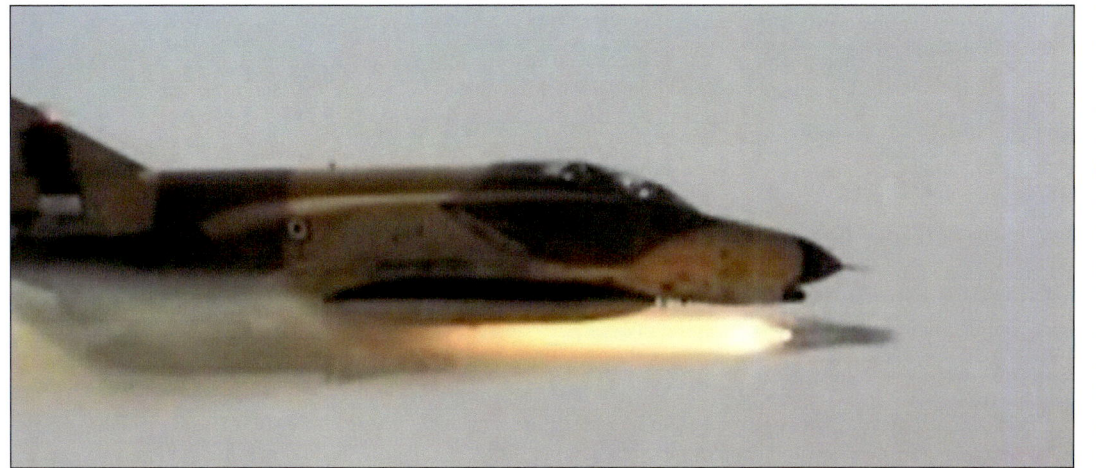

A still from a video showing an F-4E of the IRIAF firing an AGM-65A Maverick electro-optically guided air-to-ground missile. (Tom Cooper collection)

A rare photograph of IRINS *Peykan* (taken before 1979), the ship that played a crucial role in Operation Morvarid. Notable is the 76mm gun forward of the bridge, and the four canisters for BGM-84A Harpoon missiles immediately aft. She had a short, but a very intensive career. (Leon Manoucherians collection)

Major Ali-Reza Yassini, one of the pilots from TFB.6 involved in Operation Morvarid, standing in front of F-4E serial number 3-6551, one of the Phantoms known to have seen action during this battle. (Centre of Holy Defence Documents of the Navy)

around the same time that Captain Khalatbari returned to the scene during his second combat sortie of that morning:

> ...*Peykan* called two Osas escaping towards the north, in the direction of Um Qassr... I found them near the Kuwaiti island of Bubiyan and immediately sank one. During my second attack, I destroyed the other Osa as this was only 1,000 yards from the Kuwaiti coast.

The Iranians concluded that Khalatbari scored two additional hits, sinking two Iraqi missile boats: the Iraqis subsequently admitted the loss of one Osa II, and 11 of her crew (the commander and others managed to swim to shore). In turn, they claimed one Phantom shot down by SA-7s, and this loss was subsequently confirmed by the IRIAF, which declared its crew – including 1st Lieutenant Hassan Moftakhari and 2nd Lieutenant Mohammad-Kazem Roosta – missing in action. That said, repeated Iranian air strikes kept the Iraqis busy long enough for the skipper of IRINS *Joshan* to exploit this opportunity and, after picking up some of *Peykan*'s survivors, withdraw. Covered by a single ASH-3D (callsign Zireh-8), the ship managed to leave the combat zone.

Later during the afternoon, Zireh-8 – covered by a total of four F-4Es (serials 3-6564, 3-6551, 3-6623, and 3-6624, each armed with two AIM-9Js), and two F-14As of the IRIAF – returned to the scene of the battle to search for survivors of IRINS *Peykan*. Eventually, it recovered 16 sailors from the sea. Of course, this activity attracted Iraqi attention and four MiG-23MSs from No. 39 Squadron were directed over the northern Persian Gulf. This time, it was up to Captain Jalal Zandi (with 2nd Lieutenant Hossein Nik-Anjam in the back), from TFB.8, to stop them: he intercepted and shot down one Iraqi jet with a single AIM-54A fired from a range of around 30km, forcing the rest of the Iraqi formation to abort its mission. Zandi's claim was eventually confirmed: according to Iraqi sources, Lieutenant Mahmoud Mazhar from No. 39 Squadron last reported an 'air combat with Phantoms', before disappearing. His fate remains unknown.

CONCLUSIONS

Far from resulting in the 'destruction of the entire Iraqi Navy' as frequently claimed in Iran to the present day, Operation Morvarid cost Iran the following losses:

- a Kaman-class FAC, with two crewmembers killed in action and 29 missing in action
- an F-4E Phantom II from TFB.6
- three pilots of the IRIAF (including the crew of the downed Phantom and a pilot killed while acting as liaison officer aboard IRINS *Peykan*)

In turn, the Iranian action resulted in the incapacitation of Mina Khowr al-Amiyah and the ruin of Mina al-Bakr, destruction of all the heavy weaponry there, neutralisation of an entire company of Iraqi naval infantry, sinking of one P-6 and two Projeckt 205 FACs; downing of at least one, possibly up to four of MiGs and Sukhois of the Iraqi Air Force, and a total of over 100 Iraqi casualties. Moreover, during Operation Morvarid, the IRIN escorted one additional caravan to BIK and another back to Bushehr, both entirely unmolested by the enemy.

As such, this Iranian raid marked the end of the first phase in the naval war between Iran and Iraq – and resulted in a marked decrease in the activity of the Iraqi Navy: for the time being, it was 'buttoned up' inside Khowr az-Zubayr, and limited even its actions against convoys hauling 'beans, bullets, and gas' for the Iranian war effort in Khuzestan province. Operation Crocodile thus continued almost undisturbed for the rest of 1980. Indeed, hovercraft of the IRIN were also able to make regular supply runs to the Iranian garrison in Abadan – although this was now effectively besieged by the Iraqi advance. However, as time was to show, this was just the begging of a long and bloody war, which was to strain both the Iranian and Iraqi navies – and their air forces to – their maximum. That story is to be continued in Volume 2.

APPENDIX
SHIPS TRAPPED IN THE SHATT AL-ARAB, SEPTEMBER–OCTOBER 1980[1]

Ship	Displacement (grt)	Location	Notes
1 Hurizan	986	Shatt al-Arab	
7 Nissan	986	Shatt al-Arab	
14 Ramadhan	5,701	Shatt al-Arab	
Abadan Star	516	Shatt al-Arab	seriously damaged
Acpanim	??	Khorramshahr	British
Adamas	10,008	Unknown	
Aegis Baltic	12,498	Khor al-Zubair	
Agathon	10,008	Basra	
Al Hafija	???	al-Faw	sunk
Al Khalida	3,966	Shatt al-Arab	
Safina (???) Al Nasari	???	al-Faw	sunk
Al Phirosh	????	al-Faw	sunk
Al Risala	2,966	Shatt al-Arab	
Al Sabahiah	10,355	Basra	
Al-Sahil al-Arabi	5,207	Basra	
Aledressi	1,599	Basra	
Altanin or Altanieh Horizon	24,132	Khorramshahr	damaged at anchorage
Andros	15,404	Basra	later *Eleftherois*
Apus	8,365	Basra	later *Salamina*
Asia Palho	9,111	Khorramshahr	
Aurelia	5,913	Basra	
Bamburi	3,291	Khor al-Zubair	
Bolivar	9,656	Basra	
Camelia	17,040	Shatt al-Arab	sunk
Capetan Costas	8,313	Umm Qasr	
Capriolo	12,380	Khorramshahr	damaged at Jetty No. 14
Christos St. Arapakis	9,003	Basra	later *Sailflip*
Chrysalis	12,074	Shatt al-Arab	
Cynthia	10,719	Unknown	
Dimitris	8,804	Basra	
Evia	10,028	Basra	
Fedon	6,723	Basra	damaged
Fraternity	9,199	Khor al-Zubair	
Frederik Zholio-Kyuri	11,206	Umm Qasr	
Galleon Coral	9.937	Basra	
Gelaninipirpasa	????	Al-Faw	sunk
Golfo di Palermo	12,858	Basra	
Gulf Heron	8,991	Basra	
Hakozaki Maru	23,669	Umm Qasr	later *Crescent*
Ibn Al-Haitham	15,516	Umm Qasr	damaged
Inciativa	12,982	Basra	

Ship (continued)	Displacement (grt)	Location	Notes
Iran Badr	984	Khorramshahr	sunk at Jetty No. 7
Iran Bahr	870	Khorramshahr	sunk at Jetty No. 4
Iran Gheyam	8,408	Khorramshahr	badly damaged at Jetty No. 8
Iran Hejrat	10,172	Khorramshahr	badly damaged at Minoo anchorage
Iran Tarighat	???	Khorramshahr	(ex-*Arya Baz*); hydrofoil river ferry; sunk
Istranka	11,155	Basra	
Jani	8,779	Basra	
Jeptur Nagar	499	Khorramshahr	badly damaged
Jia Ling Jiang	9,870	Khorramshahr	badly damaged at Jetty No. 2
Jie Yang	??	Khorramshahr	badly damaged at Jetty No. 8
Juvena	4,891	Shatt al-Arab	
Kai Ping	10,724	Basra	
Karatachi Maru	7,073	Basra	
Khadijaan	8,856	Basra	
Khimik Zelinskly	11,206	Basra	
Khodadad Vananca	307	Khorramshahr	burned out
Kotas Mas	6,871	Shatt al-Arab	
Krasica	9,699	Khorramshahr	badly damaged
Laky	8,477	Umm Qasr	
Lika	8,771	Khorramshahr	badly damaged at Jetty No. 9
Loyalty	9,045	Basra	
Lucille	7,582	Abu Flus	
Maldive Swift	1,975	Khorramshahr	badly damaged at Jetty No. 7
Maria Sofia	9,068	Basra	
Median	???	Khorramshahr	Russian
Moajil 5	9,724	Umm Qasr	damaged
Molendo	12,490	Khorramshahr	Minoo anchorage
Mu Dan Jiang	9,541	Shatt al-Arab	
Murlindhar	???	Al-Faw	sunk
Nilkantha	2,996	Basra	
Ogden Exporter	15,601	Basra	
Olanesti	6,253	Khorramshahr	badly damaged at Jetty No. 2
Oriental Star	9,160	Shatt al-Arab	
Pearl City	5,526	Basra	
Rio Iguazu	??	Khorramshahr	escaped to the open sea
Rizcon Hong Kong	9,547	Khor al-Zubair	
Rosewood	3,292	Shatt al-Arab	
Safina al-Nasari	???	Al-Faw	
Safina al-Umar	???	Al-Faw	sunk
Santo Victor	9,983	Basra	
Saronic Sea	8,809	Basra	
Satsuki Maru	4,352	Basra	
Shree Vishnu	1,220	Shatt al-Arab	
Silver Crane	3,846	Shatt al-Arab	badly damaged
Skymnos	9,648	al-Faw	badly damaged
Steel Trader	7,606	Khorramshahr	damaged at Jetty No. 12
Strathfife	7,907	Shatt al-Arab	

Ship (continued)	Displacement (grt)	Location	Notes
Suying	4,077	Shatt al-Arab	
Taha	298	Khorramshahr	damaged on anchorage
Tenacia	11,919	Khor al-Zubair	
Timur Endeavour	5,941	Basra	broken up
Tom	8,733	Umm Qasr	
Uljanik	8,746	Khorramshahr	badly damaged at Jetty No. 1
Varuna Yan	2,999	Shatt al-Arab	damaged
Vijaya Avtar	2,353	Khorramshahr	damaged at Jetty No. 4
Wenjiang	10,922	Basra	damaged
William Holyman	1,975	Shatt al-Arab	
Wisteria	6,742	Basra	
Xanant Giant	???	Khorramshahr	
Yang Chun	8,167	Khorramshahr	damaged at Jetty No. 13
Young Statesman	11,033	Basra	later *Thalassini Idea*
Zanoobia	1,599	Shatt al-Arab	

SOURCES AND BIBLIOGRAPHY

INTERVIEWS
Major General Alwan al-Abossi (IrAF), July 2014
Major General Qaldoon Q. Bakir (IrAF), March 2007
Major General Hicham Barbouti (IrAF), August 2018
Major General Muwaffak Saeed Abdullah an-Naimi (IrAF), February 2007
Brigadier General Ahmad Sadik Rushdi al-Astrabadi (IrAF), March 2005, March 2006, March 2007 and October 2007
Babak All-e-Agha, September 2006 (son of Colonel Hashem All-e-Agha, Deputy Commander TFB.8)

PRIMARY DOCUMENTS
Written excerpts and photographs from the private documentation of the following veteran IrAF pilots were provided by Brigadier General Ahmad Sadik Rushdie al-Astrabadi:
Mohammad Ahmad
Fayez Baqir
Rabee' Dulaymi
Major General Haytham Khattab Omar (*Memoirs of the Commander of the Iraqi Air Force*, privately published, 2002)
Ahmad Sadik Rushdie al-Astrabadi, *Iraqi Air Force Electronic Warfare during the Iran-Iraq War, 1980–1988* (unpublished, 2007)
Jameel Salwan
Mohammad Salman
Mohammad Saaydon (*Pilot Memoir*, privately published, 2005)
Iraqi Air Force & Air Defence Command, *An Analytical Study on the Causes of Iraqi Aircraft Attrition During the Iran-Iraq War* (in Arabic), (self-published for internal use, May 1991; English transcription provided by Sadik)
Iraqi Air Force & Air Defence Command, *Analytical Study of Iraqi Aircraft Attrition During the Iran-Iraq War* (in Arabic), (self-published for internal use, September 1991; translation provided by Brigadier General Ahmad Sadik Rushdie al-Astrabadi)
Iraqi Air Force & Air Defence Command, *Engine-Related Problems with Su-20s, 4 September – 24 October 1980* (in Arabic), (self-published for internal use, 29 May 1981; translation provided by Brigadier General Ahmad Sadik)
Iraqi Air Force Martyrs Website, 1931–2003, iraqiairforcememorial.com
Islamic Republic of Iran Air Force, *204 KIA and 58 POW pilots of the Sacred Defence* (in Farsi), (self-published for internal use, listing 204 IRIAF pilots and crewmembers that were killed and 58 that were captured during the war with Iraq by their full rank and name, aircraft they flew, date of their death or captivity; date and place of issue unknown; copy provided by Farzin Nadimi)
Islamic Republic of Iran Navy, Centre of Holy Defence Documents of the Navy, documents as listed in endnotes
Office of Naval Intelligence (ONI), *SPEARTIP 009-88; Persian Gulf Fighter Developments*, 18 April 1988 (released in response to FOIA enquiry, October 2000)
ONI, *SPEARTIP 014-90; Iraq Fighter-Interceptor Capabilities* (date of publishing redacted; released in response to FOIA enquiry, October 2000)
ONI, *Request for Persian Gulf Related Info*, June 1987 (released in response to FOIA enquiry, October 2000)
US Department of Defence, 'Dossier on the Role of the Iraqi Air Force in the Gulf War', by the US Department of Defense sponsored Conflict Records Research Center (CRRC Record Number SH-AADF-D-000-396) in the course of 'Project Harmony')

BIBLIOGRAPHY
Abossi, Major General A., *In Memory of the Comprehensive Response* (Amman: self-published document, September 2010)
Alnasrawi, A., *The Economy of Iraq: Oil, Wars, Destruction of Development and Prospects, 1950–2010* (Westport: Greenwood Press, 1994)
British Maritime Charitable Foundation, *Why the Ships Went: Fully Quantified Analysis of the Causes of Decline of the*

United Kingdom Registered Merchant Fleet (LLP Professional Publishing, 1986)

Centre for Strategic Studies, IRIAF, *History of Air Battles, Volume 2: Invasion and First Response* (in Farsi), (Tehran: Centre for Strategic Studies, IRIAF, 2016)

Centre for Strategic Studies, IRIAF, *History of Air Battles, Volume 6: Operations Morvarid and Nasr, Air War of November and December 1980* (in Farsi), (Tehran: Centre for Strategic Studies, IRIAF, 2018)

Centre for Strategic Studies, PMO, *Supply and War Chain: The Role of the Port and Maritime Organisation* (in Farsi), (Tehran: Ports and Maritime Publications, 2008)

Cooper, T. & Sipos, M., *Iraqi Mirages: The Dassault Mirage Family in Service with the Iraqi Air Force, 1981–1988* (Warwick: Helion & Co., 2019)

Cooper, T., *MiG-23 Flogger in the Middle East: Mikoyan I Gurevich MiG-23 in Service in Algeria, Egypt, Iraq, Libya and Syria, 1973–2018* (Warwick: Helion & Co., 2018)

Cooper, T., Sadik, General de Brigade A., Bishop, F., *La guerre Iran-Irak: Les combat aériens, Hors-Serie Avions No. 22 & No. 23* (Outreau: Editions Lela Presse, 2007)

Dupuy, Col T. N. & Blanchard, Col W., *The Almanac of World Military Power* (2nd Edition) (London: Arthur Barker Ltd, 1972)

Flintham, V., *Air Wars and Aircraft: A Detailed Record of Air Combat 1945 to the Present* (London: Arms and Armour Press, 1989)

Gardiner, Robert, *Conway's All the Worlds' Fighting Ships 1947–1995* (London: Conway Maritime, 1995)

Gunston, B. & Spick, M., *Modern Air Combat: The Aircraft, Tactics and Weapons Employed in Aerial Warfare Today* (London: Salamander Books Ltd., 1983)

Gunston, B., *Modern Airborne Missiles* (London: Salamander Books Ltd., 1983)

Gunston, B., *The Illustrated Encyclopedia of the World Rockets & Missiles* (London: Salamander Books Ltd., 1979)

Gunston, B., *The Illustrated Encyclopedia of Aircraft Armament* (London: Salamander Books Ltd., 1988)

Gurbanizadeh, H., *Fire and Flight of Turtles* (in Farsi) (Tehran, Surah Mehr Publications, 2017)

Hiro, D., *The Longest War: The Iran-Iraq Military Conflict* (Routledge, Chapman and Hall Inc., 1991)

Hooton, E. R., Cooper, T. & Nadimi, F., *The Iran-Iraq War, Volume 1: The Battle for Khuzestan, September 1980 – May 1982* (Revised Edition) (Warwick: Helion & Co., 2019)

Hooton, E. R., Cooper, T. & Nadimi, F., *The Iran-Iraq War, Volume 2: Iran Strikes Back, June 1982 – December 1986* (Revised Edition) (Warwick: Helion & Co. 2019)

Hooton, E., R., Cooper, T. & Nadimi, F., *The Iran-Iraq War, Volume 3: Iraq's Triumph* (Solihull: Helion & Co., 2017)

Hooton, E., R., Cooper, T. & Nadimi, F., *The Iran-Iraq War, Volume 4: The Forgotten Fronts* (Solihull: Helion & Co., 2018)

IRIN, *Calendar of Holy Defence, Volume 6: Morvarid, Actions of the Navy from 22 November to 6 December 1980* (in Farsi) (Tehran, Office of Theoretical Research and Strategic Studies, 2011)

IRIN, *Encyclopedia of Naval Operations* (in Farsi) (Tehran: Surah Mehr Publications, 2019)

Kerdiles, J. L., *Le Super Frelon* (Outreau: Editions Lela Presse, 2012)

Lemcke, E. & Neidel, H., *Raketen über See: Die taktische Seezielrakete P-15 (Styx) im Kalten und heißen Krieg* (K. Homilius, 2008)

McLaurin, R. D., *Military Operations in the Gulf War: The Battle of Khorramshahr* (Aberdeen Proving Ground: US Army Human Engineering Laboratory, July 1982)

Mousavi, S. J., *Water and Fire: The Islamic Republic of Iran Navy Collection* (in Farsi) (Tehran: Aja Publishing, 2009)

Murray, W. & Woods, K. M., *The Iran-Iraq War: A Military and Strategic History* (Cambridge: Cambridge University Press, 2014)

Nadimi, F., *The Iranian Oil Industry and The Iran-Iraq War of 1980–88* (PhD thesis, The University of Manchester, 2011)

Navias, S. & Hooton, E. R., *Tanker Wars: The Assault on Merchant Shipping During The Iran-Iraq Conflict, 1980–1988* (New York: I. B. Tauris & Co Ltd., 1996)

O'Ballance, E., *The Gulf War* (London: Brassey's Defence Publishers, 1988)

Sadik, Brig Gen A. & Cooper, T., 'Les "Mirage" de Baghdad: les Dassault "Mirage" F1 dans la force aerienne irakienne', *Fana de l'Aviation* No. 434/2006

Sadik, Brig Gen A. & Cooper, T., 'Un Falcon 50 lance-missiles: Avion d'affaires contre navire de guerre', *Fana de l'Aviation* No. 470 (2007)

Sadik, Brig Gen A., & Cooper, T. *Iraqi Fighters, 1953–2003: Camouflage & Markings* (Houston: Harpia Publishing, 2008)

Sampson, A., *Die Waffenhändler: Von Krupp bis Lockheed, Die Geschichte eines tödlichen Geschäfts* (Reinbek bei Hamburg: Rowohl Verlag GmbH, 1977)

Shakibania, M. & Bibak, S., *Tomcat Fights* (TV documentary, Iran, 2012)

Spick, M., *Modern Fighting Aircraft: F-14 Tomcat* (London: Salamander Books Ltd., 1985)

Woods, K. M., Murray, W., Holaday, T., with Elkhamri, M., *Saddam's War: An Iraqi Military Perspective of the Iran-Iraq War* (Washington D.C.: National Defense University, 2009)

NOTES

Preface and Acknowledgements
1. Project al-Hussein involved stretching the range of the Soviet-made R-17 missile, widely known by its ASCC/NATO codename 'SS-1 Scud'. See *al-Hussein*, Middle East@War #49 for a fuller description of this and other Iraqi arms projects.
2. For details and reasons of Jakowitch's interest, see Cooper et al, *Iraqi Mirages* (details in Bibliography)

Chapter 1
1. See the Middle East@War *Military and Police Forces of the Gulf States* mini-series for further details of the security arrangements of these states.
2. DIA *Naval Forces Intelligence Study: Iran, April 1986* (DDB-1200-IR-86), pp. 11–15; Cooper et al, *Iraqi Mirages*, p. 37.
3. British Maritime Charitable Foundation, *Why the Ships Went* (LLP Professional Publishing, 1986); Ling, *Britain's Merchant Navy*
4. *Lloyds List*, 20 February 1987
5. For details on the presence of the USN in the Persian Gulf during the 1940–60s, see Palmer, pp. 46–49, 72, 82–83, 90, 94–99, and 133.
6. For details, see Palmer, pp. 81, 85–86; Hooton et al, *Desert Storm, Volume 1*, pp. 5–13, and Cooper et al, *Wings of Iraq, Volume 1*.
7. For the Soviet naval build-up in the Indian Ocean of the late 1960s and early 1970s, see alerozin.narod.ru ('Glavnaya Stranitsa 8 OPSEC: The Formation of the Indian Squadron'), and Palmer, pp. 86, 96.
8. Based on Palmer, p. 281.
9. Palmer, pp. 87–89.
10. This eviction remains controversial at the time of writing, with many of those evicted, or their descendants, claiming to have not been adequately compensated, if compensated at all.
11. *Lloyd's Shipping Registers* and Navias et al, *Tanker Wars*, pp. 14–15.
12. McLaurin, *Military Operations in the Gulf War*, p. 8.

Chapter 2
1. Gardiner, *Conway's All the World's Fighting Ships 1947–1995* (hereafter *Conway's*), pp. 183–188, 473, 589, 595, and 603; O'Ballance, pp. 14–15; DIA, *Naval Forces Intelligence Study: Iran* (DDB-1200-IR-86), pp. 2, 4–7, 10, 16, 18, 23–24, 27; *Iraq Intelligence Report: Assessing Political, Military and Economic Conditions in Iran* (SH-GMID-D-000-842); CIA/FOIA/ERR.
2. As far as is known, *Artemiz* saw little operational service during the Iran-Iraq War. In 1985, she underwent another overhaul. She received a new fire-control system, the Sea Cat launcher was removed and replaced by a SAM system of Soviet origin, and two 23mm anti-aircraft autocannons. Back to service under the new name, *Damavand*, the destroyer remained in service until 1995, and was stricken a year later.
3. In 1985, the four Vospers were renamed *Alvan, Alborz, Sabalan*, and *Sahand*, respectively.
4. Since 1940, the United States Navy has assigned sequential numerical designations to all of its aircraft, irrespective of their manufacturer or type. The sequence started with 00001: when reaching 99999 in 1945, it continued into six digits, and this remains valid to the present day. This 'Bureau Number' is assigned to every aircraft at the time of its order (not at the time it is actually delivered).
5. O'Ballance, p. 11.
6. DIA, *Naval Forces Intelligence Study: Iran*, pp. 2.
7. According to rumours making circles both within and outside Iran ever since 1978, sometime after the Empire of Iran established military cooperation with Israel in 1976, the IIN may also have placed an order for 12 Reshef-class fast missile craft. Based on the design of the German Jaguar-class of the Second World War, but using steel construction instead of wood, adding 2.4 metres (7ft 10in) to the length, and with revised internal compartmentalisation, these vessels served as predecessors to the La Combattante II-class. They were equipped with Thomson-CSF Neptune THD 1040 surveillance radar and Selenia Orion RTN-10X fire-control system, and could carry up to six Israeli-made Gabriel anti-ship missiles. Reportedly, Iran ordered 12 to be constructed in Germany, sometime in 1978, and a large number of Gabriels, but this order was cancelled – together with so many others – in February–April 1979.
8. Palmer, pp. 91–92.
9. Reportedly, Iran's interest in aircraft carriers went all the way up to the option of leasing a vessel of the USS Kitty Hawk-class (CV-63) – the last class of the conventionally-powered carriers designed and constructed for the USN – and up to 10 Knox-class ASW frigates (FF-1052). As far as can be said, nothing of this progressed any further than possible expressions of interest on the part of Tehran's representatives. However, around the same time (1977–78), Iran is known to have entered negotiations with Moscow for the purchase of six Projeckt 1124 Albatros-class anti-submarine corvettes (ASCC/NATO codename 'Grisha'): it is possible that the related talks were used to bargain for further negotiations with the USA.
10. *Conway's*, p. 186. According to the 1989 Lloyds' Casualty Return, *Iran Ajr* was eventually sold for scrap in 1989. Of interest is that a Libyan Ro-Ro was widely associated with minelaying of the Red Sea in 1983.
11. *Conway's*, p. 65.
12. The DIA reported that Tehran later approached West Germany to renew the contract for the Type 209 submarines, but that the Germans refused to deliver until the end of the war with Iraq. See, *Naval Forces Intelligence Study: Iran*, p. 10.
13. O'Ballance, pp. 20, 23; Pivka, p. 97. Notably, the DIA claimed that the navy's officer corps was largely opposed to the regime, 'but remained for nationalist reasons' (see DIA, *Naval Forces Intelligence Study: Iran*, pp. 6, 8). This stands in stark contrast to reports by Iranian naval officers interviewed over the years (see below for details).

Chapter 3
1. This sub-chapter is based on *Conway's*, pp. 188–189, 412, 416–420; Cordesman et al, pp. 70, 102; Khafaji et al, *Dawr al-Quwa al-Bahriya al-Iraqiya fee al-Harb al-Iraqiya al Iraniya*, p. 69; O'Ballance, pp. 29, 72; Malovany, pp. 26, 85–86, 814–817; Murray et al, *The Iran-Iraq War*, p. 69; Pavlov, pp. 154–155; 170, 175–176, 184–185, 193–195, 202–203, 274, 300; Pivka, p. 103, Woods, *Saddam's Generals*, pp. 153–159, and DIA, *Military Intelligence Summary, Volume III, Part II* (DDB-2680-103-88), pp. 21–24.
2. Notably, Russian sources of reference (repeated by German sources, like Lemcke et al), report deliveries of only four Projekt-205 FACs to Iraq, all starting in 1974.
3. *Conway's*, pp. 188 & O'Ballance, pp. 29, 72.
4. For a detailed and illustrated history of the IrAF in the 1970s, see Sipos et al, *Wings of Iraq, Volume 2*.
5. Conclusions based on the study of available photographs of Iraqi Super Frelons.
6. Kerdiles, *Le Super Frelon*.
7. For additional details on Iraq's acquisition of Su-22s, No. 109 Squadron, and Barbouti, see Sipos et al, *Wings of Iraq, Volume 2*.

Chapter 4
1. Unless stated otherwise, this sub-chapter is based on transcription of IRIN, *Plan Abouzar*, 1 December 1979; IRIAF, *Plan Entegham*, 1 December 1979; IRIN, *Plan Zolfaghar*, 16 June 1980 & McLaurin, *Military Operations in the Gulf War*, p. 9.
2. During the reign of the Shah, Iran had only one intelligence and security agency: SAVAK (*Sezeman-e Ettalaat va Amniat-e Keshvar*, or 'Intelligence and Security Organisation of the Country') – which emerged from the former Second Bureau of the Imperial Iranian Army, and always maintained very close relations to the armed forces. Officially at least, SAVAK was closed down shortly before the Shah left Iran, in late January 1979. Reportedly, more than 3,000 of its staff were targeted for reprisals by the new regime in Tehran, which disbanded the organisation. Actually, the bulk of SAVAK remained intact and operational, and was subsequently even expanded under a minimally changed designation: SAVAMA (*Sazeman-e Ettalaat va Amniat-e Melli-e Iran*, or 'Intelligence and Security Organisation of the Country').
3. Unless stated otherwise, this sub-chapter is based on transcriptions of IRIN, *Emergency Shipping Movement Control Plan for the*

Persian Gulf, 18 April 1980; IRIN, *Fighting Directive Peykan*, 18 April 1980 and IRIN, *Document 1*, 18 April 1980.
4. IRIN, *Document 590127041*, 23 September 1980, Centre of Holy Defence Documents of the Navy & IRIN, *Loss of Hovercraft in Khosrow Abad*, 10 October 1980. Indicating how seriously the IRIN considered the threat of an Iraqi invasion as of April 1980, earlier that month its HQ initiated Operation Derafah. Essentially, this resulted in the evacuation of two BH.7-class hovercraft from their base on Khark Island to Naval Station Bandar Abbas – with a refuelling stop at Kish Island (IRIN, *Document 590124028*, 12 April 1980, Centre of Holy Defence Documents of the Navy).
5. Sadik, 03/2005 & CIA, *Iran-Iraq: Determining Who Started the Iran-Iraq War*, 25 November 1987, CIA/FOIA/ERR. One of the paradoxes of Iraq under Saddam is that while Tehran did manage to establish underground political networks and a few expatriate groups that opposed the Ba'ath regime in Iraq, the Iranians were never able to gain any popular support among the Iraqi Shi'a. Nevertheless, the related Iranian activity made not only Saddam, but also many top Iraqi military commanders – the majority of whom were Sunni – generally suspicious of the Shi'a, regardless how loyal to Baghdad they proved to be.
6. For a detailed description of the operations in question, see Hooton et al, *Iran-Iraq War, Volume 4*.
7. For details on related Iraqi preparations, see Hooton et al, *Iran-Iraq War, Volume 1*.
8. Woods et al, *Saddam's War*, p. 32. Precise details of what exactly happened on 4 September 1980 on the border between Iran and Iraq remain elusive. The Iraqi media (for example *Baghdad Observer*, on 7 September 1980) originally reported a 'severe artillery attack' on – literally – two villages. However, subsequently, this affair was styled as 'the first day of the Iranian aggression', and the Iranians were accused of 'bombing and shelling Iraqi cities and towns', including Baghdad, and 'killing women and children'. Sufficient to say that there is no evidence that anything of this kind ever happened. Nevertheless, most Iraqi sources interviewed over time consider this day – 4 September 1980 – as 'the day the Iran-Iraq War began'.
9. Unless stated otherwise, based on transcription of IRIN, *Task Force 421*, 17 September 1980.
10. Hooton et al, *Iran-Iraq War, Volume 1*, pp. 17–19. The pilot of the Mi-25 apparently managed an emergency landing before succumbing to his wounds; the subsequent fate of his mount and that of the other crewmembers remains unknown. The pilots of the MiG-21R and the Su-22 were both killed in action.
11. Woods, pp. 154–155. Woods' conclusion is based on an interview with Lieutenant General Abid Mohammed al-Kabi, Director of Training, Iraqi Navy, as of 1980, and its commander from 1982 onwards.
12. For details on Iraqi acquisition of MiG-23MS and the operations of No. 39 Squadron as of 1976–80, see Cooper, *MiG-23 Flogger in the Middle East* and Sipos et al, *Wings of Iraq, Volume 2*.
13. In addition to warships listed in this table, the IRIN had a number of light logistic ships, distributed as follows:
    - 1st Naval District: four Soro-class
    - 2nd Naval District: three Soro-class
    - 3rd Naval District: three light auxiliary ships (*Lavan, Hormuz*, and *Kish*)

Chapter 5

1. IrAF, *Analytical Study*, p. 3; Sadik, 03/2005; Woods, *Saddam's Generals*, pp. 207–210. There is little doubt that some points were the result of the general sloppiness of Iraqi preparations, but also of overwhelming secrecy. Not only Sadik, but also several other generals interviewed by Woods et al stressed that the IrAF received the plans for the attack on 22 September 1980 only one or two days earlier, and then in the form of a plan for a 'training exercise'. Unsurprisingly, the Iraqi military went into that war without a strategic concept, without ideas about strategic and operational aims and implications, and without an operational and tactical focus: indeed, many of its top commanders seem to have shared Saddam's hopes that their invasion would collapse Iran on its own, 'one way or the other'.
2. Unless stated otherwise, this sub-chapter is based on transcriptions of the reports IRIN, *Loss of PBR 265 on Arvand Road*, 19 September 1980; IRIN, and *Loss of AB 212 ASW (Number 411)*, 20 September 1980. According to the first of these reports, the crew of the PBR Mk III, hull number 265, that was machine-gunned by the Iraqis in cold blood, included:
    - Lieutenant (Junior Grade) Akbar Taghizadeh (CO)
    - Petty Officer Esmaeeil Taj Bakht (Artillery)
    - Petty Officer Mohammad Reza Parviz Zadeh (Engineer; whose body was never found)
    - Petty Officer Mansour Dos (Electronics)
    - Petty Officer Jamshid Ghahraki (Engineer)
    - Petty Officer Sayed Kazem Taherik (from IRINA)
    - Lieutenant (Junior Grade) Koroush Shahbazi (from the Marines)
    - Sergeant Major Mohammad Reza Ali Poor (Electronics, from the Army)
3. IRIN, *Document 590901193*, 23 September 1980, Centre of Holy Defence Documents of the Navy.
4. Khafaji, pp. 119–130, 132, 134–146; Khafaji et al, pp. 119–130, 132, 134–146; Malovany, pp. 101, 130, 142–143, 178, 224–225, 246, 232; Murray et al, pp. 200–201 & O'Ballance, pp. 45–46.
5. Unless stated otherwise, this and the following sub-chapters are based on Sazman, *Iran-Iraq War*, pp. 45–97.
6. It was only after the war that Lloyds List International announced that a total of 14 vessels trapped in the Umm Qasr area of the Khowr az-Zubayr had managed to get out of the war zone.
7. Gurbanzadeh, *Fire and Flight of Turtles* (based on memoirs of hovercraft pilot Mir Mansour Seyed Qureshi), IRIN, *Document 590630060*, no date available, Centre of Holy Defence Documents of the Navy; IRIN, *Encyclopaedia of Naval Operations*, pp. 90–91.

Chapter 6

1. Unless started otherwise, based on transcription of IRIN, *Fighting Directive Azhdar*, 23 September 1980.
2. Based on transcription of IRIN, *Loss of Phantom of TFB.6 Bushehr*, 26 September 1980.
3. Based on transcription of IRIN, *Loss of two Phantoms of TFB.6 Bushehr*, 27 September 1980.
4. Based on transcription of IRIN, Investigation into Loss of Three Phantoms of TFB.6 Bushehr, 30 September 1980.
5. Unless stated otherwise, this sub-chapter is based on transcription of IRIN, *Directive Behroz*, 30 September 1980.
6. Transcription of IRIN, *Report on Presence of P205 Osa in Kuwait*, 10 October 1980.
7. Unless stated otherwise, this sub-chapter is based on transcriptions of IRIN, *Attacks on MS Navid and Tug Payam*, 16 October 1980 and IRIN, *Sinking of Mehran*, 18 October 1980. Notably, the survivors reported that both *Navid* and *Payam* were attacked by 'air strike' while about five miles south of the buoy at the entrance to Khowr al-Mousa. However, the attack took place at the sunset, and Iraqis flew no nocturnal operations at the time. Baghdad claimed the sinking of two 'Kaman-class missile boats', but never mentioned the means.
8. On return to TFB.6, Dowran was informed that he had hit an Iranian warship and killed several of its crewmembers. Aghast at this mistake, Dowran not only quit flying but became a drug-addict and was away from operations for several months. Indeed, it is possible that this negative experience left a lasting impact upon his subsequent career, including his last mission against a target in the Baghdad area, where he was shot down and killed in 1982. Ironically, the regime in Tehran subsequently created all sorts of legends about Abbas Dowran, converting him into a national hero.
9. Unless stated otherwise, this sub-chapters is based on transcription of IRIN, *Sinking of P205 Osa by IRINS Joshan*, 31 October 1980.

Chapter 7

1. Sadik, interview, 03/2005 and Woods, p. 157. Notably, Kabi claimed the deployment of an entire battalion of the Iraqi naval infantry on the two loading terminals, but the two did not offer enough space for this many troops. More likely, one of the battalions of the 77th Naval Infantry Brigade was rotating one of its three companies.

2. Unless stated otherwise, this sub-chapter is based on transcription of IRIN, *Operation Ashkan*, 2 November 1980.
3. Unless stated otherwise, this sub-chapter is based on transcription of IRIN, *Operation Morvarid*, 30 November 1980; Khafaji et al, pp. 130–131; Centre for Strategic Studies, *History of Air Battles*, Vol.6, pp. 64–71 & Malovany, pp. 142–143.
4. Sadik, interview, 03/2005; Khafaji et al, pp. 130–131 & Malovany, pp. 142–143.
5. Unless stated otherwise, this sub-chapter is based on transcription of IRIN, *Operation Morvarid*, 30 November 1980; Centre for Strategic Studies, *History of Air Battles*, Vol.6, pp. 64–71, 102; IRIN, *Morvarid*, p. 186; Sadik, interview, 03/2005; Khafaji et al, pp. 130–131 & Malovany, pp. 142–143.
6. No corresponding losses of the IrAF are known. However, it is possible that one of the Iranian claims in question is related to an episode that became the subject of legends within the IrAF, and was provided by Brigadier General Ahmad Sadik Rushdie al-Astrabadi (interview, 03/2005). Correspondingly, in a clash that occurred 'sometime in November 1980', an Iranian AIM-54As narrowly missed a Su-22 of No. 109 Squadron. Triggered by proximity fuse, the warhead went off, but not closely enough to destroy the target. The jet was set on fire, but the Iraqi pilot managed to land safely at Wahda AB. Arguably, by then, the Sukhoi was so badly damaged by fire that it was eventually written off. However, from that time onwards the majority of IrAF officers and pilots became convinced that this type was superior to anything else in service with this air force and, de-facto, impossible to replace. This became the primary reason why the IrAF continued buying additional fighter-bombers of this family throughout the rest of the 1980s.

Appendix
1. Based on Navias et al, pp. 33–34 and amended by Ted Hooton with data from *Lloyd's Casualty Returns*, 1989–1993.

ABOUT THE AUTHORS

TOM COOPER
Tom Cooper is an Austrian aerial warfare analyst and historian. Following a career in the worldwide transportation business – during which he established a network of contacts in the Middle East and Africa – he moved into narrow-focus analysis and writing on small, little-known air forces and conflicts, about which he has collected extensive archives. This has resulted in specialisation in Middle Eastern, African and Asian air forces. He has authored and co-authored more than a dozen books about the Iran-Iraq War, including four volumes on ground warfare, several about the Iranian air force, two about the history of the Iraqi Air Force, and one on the history of operational deployment Dassault Mirage F.1s in Iraq. Cooper has been an editor of Helion's five @War series since 2017.

SIROUS EBRAHIMI
Sirous Ebrahimi, from Iran, is a sailor, captain in the Iranian merchant navy and a marine pilot. Born into a military family, he became interested in the history of aviation and air forces during the childhood. In his youth, he participated in the Iran-Iraq War and took part in the battles of East Basra and Shalamcheh. After the war, he engaged in commercial shipping, and obtained valuable, first-hand experience in the field of defence. He has written several books summarising his war memoirs and numerous articles published in the specialised press in Iran.

E R HOOTON
E.R. (Ted) Hooton is a retired defence journalist who worked for 30 years with Moench and Jane's before establishing the Spyglass newsletters. Since retirement he has focussed upon military history and has written some 15 books covering subjects as diverse as the Iran-Iraq Tanker War (co-authored with Mr Martin Navias), the Chinese Civil War, the Luftwaffe, the Balkan Wars (1912-1913), the Spanish Civil War, Air Operations over the Western Front (1916-1918) and Eastern Front (1941-1945). With Tom Cooper he has written a four-volume history of the Iran-Iraq War on the ground for Helion's @War series.